Sir John Fortescue's
The Red Path

Sir John Fortescue's
The Red Path

A History of the British Army During the
French and Indian Wars

J. W. Fortescue

LEONAUR

Sir John Fortescue's The Red Path
A History of the British Army During the French and Indian Wars
by J. W. Fortescue

FIRST EDITION

First published under the title
A History of the British Army Vol 2 (Extract)

Leonaur is an imprint of Oakpast Ltd

Copyright in this form © 2014 Oakpast Ltd

ISBN: 978-1-78282-359-9 (hardcover)
ISBN: 978-1-78282-360-5 (softcover)

http://www.leonaur.com

Publisher's Notes

Contents

CHAPTER 1

The Barbarous Inroads

The English claim to the sovereignty of North America dated from the reign of Henry the Seventh, (1457-1509), under whose patronage Sebastian Cabot, (1481-1557), had made his great discoveries; but it was the Spaniards who first approached the unknown land and gave it the name of Florida, and it was a Frenchman, Denis of Honfleur, who first explored the Gulf of St. Lawrence. So also it was a Frenchman, Jacques Cartier, who gave its name to that noble river, and the name of Mount Royal or Montreal to the hill on which the city now stands. Full sixty years passed away before further attempt was made to found European settlements on the North American continent, and then English and French took the work in hand well-nigh simultaneously.

In 1603 De Monts obtained permission from the French king to colonise Acadia, [1] discovered and planted the harbour called by him Port Royal and by the English at a later date Annapolis Royal, and explored the coast southward as far as that Plymouth where the Pilgrim Fathers were to land in 1621. The attempt of De Monts was a failure, and it was left to Samuel Champlain to begin the work anew by the founding of Quebec and by the establishment of Montreal at once as a gateway for Indian trade and a bulwark against Indian invasion. To him was due the exploration of the River Richelieu and of the lake which bears his name, as far as the two headlands which were afterwards to become famous under the names of Ticonderoga and Crown Point. In Champlain's wake followed the Jesuit missionaries, whose history presents so curious a mixture of that which is highest and lowest in human nature. Lastly, to Champlain must be ascribed not only the final settlement of the French in Canada but the initia-

---

1. Acadia is, and always was, a vague geographical term. The name when first used comprised the territory between latitude 40 and 46.

tion of the French policy of meddling with the internal politics of the Indian tribes.

Meanwhile an English Company of Adventurers for Virginia had established a first settlement on the James river, just three-and-twenty years after Raleigh's abortive attempt to accomplish the same feat. The rival nations had not been settled in North America five years before they came into collision. The English claimed the whole continent in virtue of Cabot's discoveries, and the English Governor of Virginia enforced the claim by sending a ship to Acadia, which demolished the Jesuit settlement at Port Royal and carried the prisoners to Jamestown.

A few years later a Scottish nobleman, Sir William Alexander, afterwards Earl of Stirling, obtained a grant from James the First of the territory which, in compliment to his native land, he christened Nova Scotia, and planted a colony there. Finally, in 1627, during the war with France, a company of London merchants, inspired chiefly by two brothers named Kirke, sent an expedition up the St. Lawrence, which captured Quebec, established settlements in Cape Breton, and in a word made the conquest of Canada. Unfortunately, however, Charles the First, then as always impecunious, allowed these important acquisitions to be restored to France at the Peace of 1632 for the paltry sum of fifty thousand pounds. The conquering merchants protested but in vain, pleading passionately for the retention at any rate of Quebec. They wrote:

> If the king keep it we do not care what the French or any other can do, though they have an hundred sail of ships and ten thousand men. [2]

So truly was appreciated, even in the seventeenth century, the strategic value of that famous and romantic fortress.

Still even so Acadia[3] was not yet permanently lost, for in 1654 Major Sedgwicke, who had been sent by Cromwell to attack the Dutch settlements on the Hudson, took the opportunity to capture the French ports at St. Johns, Port Royal and Penobscot, and restored Acadia to England once more. With England it remained until 1667, when it was finally made over to France by the Treaty of Breda. Thus was established the French dominion in what is now called Canada.

Meanwhile, in the same year as had seen the first British settle-

---

2. *Cal. S. P., Col.*, 1632.
3. Acadia included Nova Scotia and more.

ment in Nova Scotia, English emigrants had landed at New Plymouth and founded the New England which was destined to swallow up New France. King James granted the infant settlement a charter of incorporation, encouraged it, and in 1625 declared by proclamation that the territories of Virginia and New England should form part of his empire. [4] The next step was the foundation of a distinct colony at Massachusetts Bay in 1628, which was erected into a corporation two years later and soon increased to a thousand persons. In 1635 yet another settlement was formed at Connecticut by emigrants from Massachusetts; and in the same year the intolerance of his fellow-settlers in Massachusetts drove Roger Williams afield to found the colony of Rhode Island.

Finally, in 1638, another secession brought about the establishment of New Haven. The settlers had left England, as they pleaded, to find liberty of conscience; but as the majority understood by this phrase no more than licence to coerce the consciences of others, the few that really sought religious liberty wandered far before they found it.

A very few years sufficed to assure the preponderance of Massachusetts in the Northern Colonies. It widened its borders, absorbed the scattered settlements of New Hampshire and Maine, and in 1644 took its place at the head of the four federated colonies of New England.[5] The distraction caused by the Civil War in Britain left the colonies practically free from all control by the mother country, and Massachusetts seized the opportunity to erect a theocracy, which was utterly at variance with the terms of her charter, and to assume, together with the confederacy of New England, the airs and privileges of an independent State.

The ambitious little community coined her own money, negotiated with the French in Acadia without reference to England, refused to trade with other colonies that were loyal to the king's cause, resented the appointment by the Long Parliament of Commissioners for the administration of the colonies, and hinted to Cromwell that the side which she might take in the Dutch war of 1653 would depend entirely on the treatment which she might receive from him. As her reward she received the privilege of exemption from the restrictions of the Navigation Acts.

Then came the Restoration; and the confederacy of New England

---

4. The boundaries of New England were defined by the fortieth and forty-fifth degrees of latitude.
5. Massachusetts, New Haven, Plymouth, Connecticut.

quickly fell to pieces. Connecticut received a separate charter, under which she absorbed New Haven; and Rhode Island obtained a separate charter likewise. Massachusetts being thus left isolated, Charles the Second determined to inquire into the many complaints made against her of violation of her charter. The colonists replied by setting their militia in order as if for armed resistance; but on reconsideration decided to fall back on smooth words, false promises, false statements, and skilful procrastination. Such methods might seem at first sight to be misplaced in a community of saints, such as Massachusetts boasted herself to be, but at least they were never employed without previous invocation of the Divine guidance. For twenty years the colonists contrived to keep the Royal authority at arm's length, till at last, after long forbearance on the side of Whitehall, the charter was cancelled by legal process, and Massachusetts was restored to her dependence on the mother country.

In the course of these years the English settlements in North America had multiplied rapidly. Maryland had been granted to Lord Baltimore in 1632; Carolina was planted by a company in 1663; Delaware with New Jersey was assigned by patent to the Duke of York, afterwards James the Second, in 1664, and Pennsylvania to William Penn in 1680. In fact, by the close of Charles the Second's reign the British seaboard in North America extended from the river St. Croix [6] in the north to the river Savannah in the south. But of all England's acquisitions during this period the most momentous was that of the Dutch settlements on the Hudson, captured in 1664 by Colonel Nicolls, who gave to the town of New Amsterdam its now famous name of New York. [7]

One chief advantage of New York was that it possessed a direct way to the west from Albany, on the Hudson, up the Mohawk River to Lake Oneida and so to Lake Ontario, whereby it had access to the great fur-trade with the Indians. But this consideration, important though it was commercially, paled before the strategical significance of the port of New York. No more simple method of explaining this can be found than to quote the belief held by many of the English emigrants before they sailed, that New England was an island. In a

---

6. The English always laid claim to the country as far north as the St Croix; the French, on the other hand, claimed it as far south as the Kennebec. This difference as to the true boundary of Acadia was one of the many points of friction between the two nations. 7. It was recaptured by the Dutch in 1673 but restored to England by the treaty of 1674.

sense this is almost true, the country being surrounded by the sea, to north, east, and south, and by the rivers Hudson and St. Lawrence to the west. Champlain had already paddled up the Richelieu to Lake Champlain with the design of passing through Lake George, carrying his canoes to the headwaters of the Hudson and re-embarking for a voyage down the river to the sea. He had in fact chosen the highway of lakes and rivers on which the principal battles for the possession of the New World were to be fought. The northern key of that highway was Quebec, the southern New York. France possessed the one, and England the other. The power that should hold both would hold the whole continent.

Let us now turn for a moment to the proceedings of the French during these same years. Unlike the English, who stuck sedulously to the work of making their settlement self-supporting by agriculture, they were intent rather on trading with the Indians for fur and exploring the vast territory which lay to south and west of them. To these objects may be added the salvation of the souls of the Indian tribes; for beyond all doubt it was zeal for the conversion, or at any rate for the baptism, of these savages that led the Jesuits through endless hardship and danger into the heart of the continent. As early as 1613 Champlain had travelled up the Ottawa by way of Lake Nipissing and French River to Lake Huron, returning by Lake Simcoe and Lake Ontario. Jesuit missionaries followed the same track in 1634, and established a mission on the peninsula that juts out from the eastern shore of Lake Huron.

From thence they spread to Lakes Superior and Michigan, erecting mission-houses and taking possession of vast tracts of land and water in the name of King Louis the Fourteenth. Shortly after the restoration of King Charles the Second, Jean Talon, Intendant of Canada, formed the resolution of getting in rear of the English settlements and confining the settlers to a narrow strip of the sea-board; his plan being to secure the rivers that formed the highways of the interior, and to follow them, if they should prove to flow thither, to the Gulf of Mexico, so as to hold both British and Spaniards in check. A young adventurer, named Robert Lasalle, appeared at the right moment as a fit instrument to his hand.

In 1670 Lasalle passed through the strait, still called Detroit, which leads from Lake Huron to Lake Erie, reached a branch of the Ohio and made his way for some distance down that river. Three years later a Jesuit, Joliet, striking westward from the western shore of Lake

Michigan, descended the Wisconsin and followed the Mississippi to the junction of the Arkansas. In 1678 an expedition under Lasalle explored the passage from Lake Ontario to Lake Erie, and discovered the Falls of Niagara, where Lasalle, with immediate appreciation of the strategic value of the position, proceeded to build a fort.

Finally, in 1680, Lasalle penetrated from the present site of Chicago on Lake Michigan to the northern branch of the River Illinois, paddled down to the Mississippi, and after five months of travel debouched into the Gulf of Mexico. He took nominal possession of all the country through which he passed; and the vast territory between the Alleghanies and the Rocky Mountains from the Rio Grande and the Gulf of Mexico to the uppermost waters of the Missouri were annexed to the French crown under the name of Louisiana.

The next step was to secure the advantages that should accrue from the discoveries of Lasalle. To this end the fort at Niagara had already been built; and Fort Frontenac was next erected at the northern outlet of Lake Ontario to cut off the English from trade with the Indians. At the strait of Michillimackinac, between Lakes Huron and Michigan, a Jesuit mission sufficiently provided for the same object. Besides these there were established Fort Miamis by the south-eastern shore of Lake Michigan, to bar the passage from the lake to the Upper Illinois, Fort St. Louis, near the present site of Utica, to secure the trade with the tribes on the plains of the Illinois, and yet another fort on the Lower Mississippi.

Such a monopoly of the Indian trade was by no means to the taste of the British and Dutch, nor of the Five Indian Nations, better known by the French name of Iroquois, whom they had taken under their special protection. Nevertheless, in their simple plodding industry, their zeal for religious controversy and their interminable squabbles over their boundaries, the English colonies took little heed to what was going on in the continent behind them. One man alone saw the danger from the first, namely, Colonel Thomas Dongan, an officer who had begun his career in the French army, but had left it for the British, and after some service at Tangier had been sent out as Governor to New York.

Dongan, however, was at first unsupported either by the Government at Whitehall or by the neighbouring colonies. His protests were vigorous to discourtesy, but he had small means for enforcing them. One resource indeed he did possess, namely the friendship of the Iroquois, who were the dominant tribes of the continent; for with all their subtle policy and their passion for interference with native affairs, the French had never succeeded in alienating the Iroquois—who covered the flank of New York and New England towards Canada from their alliance with the British. Dongan therefore assiduously cultivated a good understanding with these Indians against the moment when he should be allowed to act.

Meanwhile the French went yet further in aggression. They destroyed the factories of the Hudson's Bay Company; they treacherously entrapped and captured a number of Iroquois at Fort Frontenac, plundered English traders, and repaired and strengthened the fort built by Lasalle at Niagara. Dongan's indignation rose to a dangerous height; and now at last came a reply from England to his previous reports, and an order to repel further aggression on the Iroquois by force. Assembling a force of local militia at Albany he first insisted on the destruction of the fort at Niagara; and then the Iroquois burst in upon Canada and spread terror to the very gates of Montreal. It was just at this crisis that William of Orange displaced James the Second on the throne of England, and that war broke out between England and France. Therewith New England and New France entered upon a conflict which was to last with little intermission for the next seventy years.

Judging from mere numbers the contest between the rival colonies should have been short, for the population of New England was over ninety thousand, whereas that of Canada did not exceed twelve thousand. But this disparity was more than equalised by other advantages of the French. In the first place, they were compact, united, and under command of one man, who was an able and experienced soldier. In the second, a large proportion of the inhabitants had undergone long military training, the French king offering bounties both of money and of land to officers and soldiers who should consent to remain in the colony. The chief delight of the male population was not the tilling of the soil; they loved rather to hunt and fish, and live the free and fascinating life of an Indian in the forest. Every man therefore was a skilful woodsman, a good marksman, a handy canoe-man, and in a word admirably trained for forest fighting. Finally, there was a permanent garrison of regular troops, which never fell below, and very often exceeded, fifteen hundred men.

The English settler, on the other hand, knew little of the forest. When not engaged in husbandry he was a fisherman in his native heritage, the sea. Every colony had its own militia, which legally included, as a rule, the whole male population between the ages of sixteen and sixty. In the early days of North American settlement the colonists had been at pains to bring with them trained officers who could give them instruction in the military art. Such an officer was Miles Standish, who had served with the English troops in the Dutch service; such another was Captain John Underhill, who had fought in Ireland, Spain, and the Low Countries, and was reputed a friend of Maurice of Nassau. Under such leaders, in 1637, seventy-seven colonists had boldly attacked an encampment of four hundred Indian warriors and virtually annihilated them; giving, in fact, as fine an exposition of the principles of savage warfare as is to be found in our history.[8] In 1653 again, New England, once assured of Cromwell's favour, made great and expensive preparations for an attack on the Dutch; and Massachusetts supplied two hundred volunteers to Nicolls for the capture of New York in 1664.

But as time went on the military efficiency of the colonies decreased; and in the war against the Indian chief, Philip, in 1671, the settlers suffered disaster upon disaster. The officers possessed neither skill nor knowledge; and the men, though they showed no lack of bravery and tenacity, were wholly innocent of discipline. Moreover, they shared the failing of the English militia of the same period, that they were unwilling to go far from their own homes. Again, since the confederacy of New England had been broken up, the jealousy and selfishness of the several provinces had weakened them for military efficiency. In the great peril of 1671 Rhode Island, being full of Quakers, would not move a finger to help her neighbours, and Connecticut, exasperated by extreme provocation, actually armed herself a few years later to inflict punishment on the cantankerous little community.[9]

Within the several provinces again there was no great unanimity, and in fact in the event of a war with France every advantage of skill, of unity, and of prompt and rapid action lay with the French. James the Second, who saw the peril of the situation, tried hard to mend matters during his brief reign by uniting New England, New York, and New Jersey under the rule of a single governor, Sir Edmund Andros, an officer of the Guards. The experiment from one point of view was statesmanlike enough, but as it could not be tried without abolishing

---

8. The reader may also recall the case of Whalley the regicide, who fled to Massachusetts after the Restoration. See the Note to *Scott's Peveril of the Peak,* chap. 4.
9. Palfrey. *History of New England,* vol. iii.

the representative assemblies of the various states, it defeated its own object by its extreme unpopularity.

The military aid furnished to the American colonies from home throughout this early period was infinitesimal. New England had never appealed to the mother country for help even in her utmost need. An independent company of regular troops was formed for the garrison of New York while the Duke of York was proprietor, and another company was also maintained for a short time in Virginia; but the first troops of the standing army to visit America were a mixed battalion of the First and Coldstream Guards, which crossed the Atlantic to suppress the Virginian rebellion of 1677. When Andros assumed his government in 1686 he brought with him a second company of soldiers from England. These were the first red-coats ever seen in Boston, and they have the credit of having taught New England to "drab, drink, blaspheme, curse and damn." Thus though the militia of the colonies under Andros might muster a nominal total of ten or twelve thousand men, these two companies were all that he could have brought to meet the thirty-two or more companies of regular troops in Montreal and Quebec.

The outbreak of the war in 1689 brought back an efficient soldier, Count Frontenac, to the government of Canada. He knew the country well, having already served there as governor from 1672 to 1682, and in that capacity seconded the great designs of Lasalle. On his arrival he at once made preparations for an advance on Albany by Lakes Champlain and George and for a rapid movement against New York. The project fortunately issued in no more than a general massacre of the inhabitants on the northern frontier of New York; but when that province called in alarm upon New England for assistance, it was found that Massachusetts had risen in revolution at the news of King James's fall, had imprisoned Andros, and through sheer perversity had cancelled all his military dispositions for the protection of New Hampshire and Maine. The Indians accordingly swept down upon the defenceless borders and made frightful havoc with fire and sword.

In the following year the colonies of New York and New England met in congress and agreed to make a counter -stroke against Canada. More remarkable still, Massachusetts for the first time appealed to England for military aid in the furtherance of this enterprise; though, as may be guessed by those who have followed me through the story of King William's difficulties, the appeal was perforce rejected. The colonies therefore resolved to act alone, and despatched fifteen hundred troops by the usual line of inland waterways against Montreal, and thirty-two ships under Sir William Phips against Quebec. The expedition by land soon broke down on its way through dissension, indiscipline, and disease; and the fleet, though it made an easy conquest of Acadia, failed miserably before Quebec.

The next year a small force from New York made a second futile raid into Canada; but for the most part the English colonies were content to hound on their Indian allies against the French. The French on their side retaliated in kind, and, as circumstances gave them opportunity, with still greater barbarity. Hundreds of defenceless settlers on the border were thus slaughtered without the slightest military advantage. Frontenac wrote repeated letters to his master urging him to determine the possession of the continent once for all by sending a fleet to capture New York; but either Louis's hands were too full or he failed to appreciate the wisdom of Frontenac's counsel, for in any case, fortunately, he left New York unmolested.

The sphere of operations widened itself over Acadia and Newfoundland, and the war dragged on in a desultory fashion with raid and counter-raid, generally to the advantage of the French. To the last the English colonies were blind to the importance of the issue at stake. Jealous, self-centred, and undisciplined, many of them took no part whatever in the war; two only, New England and New York, rose to aggressive action, which, though the stroke was wisely aimed against the tap-root of French power, failed utterly from lack of organisation and discipline. The French struck always at strategic points where their blow would tell with full force and weight. The colonists in their insane jealousy of the crown neglected the defence of these strategic points simply because it was enjoined by the mother country, and refused to provide the contingents of troops requested by the English commander-in-chief. [10] In fine, when the Peace of Ryswick ended the war, the French could reckon that they had achieved one great success; they had broken the power of the most formidable of the Indians, the Iroquois.

Massachusetts, which had suffered heavily from the war, found her-

---

10. The contingents were Massachusetts, 350 men; Virginia, 250; Maryland, 160; Connecticut, 120; Rhode Island, 48; Pennsylvania, 80; Virginia and Maryland commuted their obligations for a sum of money. Parkman. *Frontenac.* (*Musket & Tomahawk,* a Military History of the French & Indian War, 1753-1760, and *Redcoat & Warpaint,* a Military History of Pontiac's War, 1760-1765 by Francis Parkman are also published by Leonaur.)

self at its close obliged once more to invoke the assistance of England. In an address to the king she prayed for his orders to the several colonial governments to give their assistance against French and Indians, for a supply of ammunition, for the protection of a fleet, and for aid in the reduction of Canada, "the unhappy fountain," as they wrote, "from which issue all our miseries." So far, therefore, the war had taught one useful lesson; but, indeed, even at the time of her greatest disloyalty to the English crown Massachusetts had always soundly hated the French. Obviously closer union of the colonies for military purposes could not but be for the general advantage, and sundry schemes were prepared to promote it; but all alike were unsuccessful, though nothing could be more certain than that further trouble was ahead.

The renewal of war in 1702 brought the usual raids of Indians, stirred up by the French, upon the borders of the English colonies. These barbarous inroads, which meant the massacre and torture of innocent settlers, could serve no military end except to commit the Indians to hostility with the English, and naturally aroused the fiercest resentment. The colonies, however, once again showed neither unity nor zeal for the common cause. New York evinced an apathy which was little short of criminal, Connecticut long held aloof, Rhode Island only after infinite haggling supplied grudging instalments of men and money. Massachusetts alone, true to her traditions, showed some vigour and spirit and actually made an attack on Port Royal in Acadia, choosing that point because it could be reached by sea. The expedition, however, failed with more than usual discredit owing to ignorance and unskilfulness in the commanders and utter indiscipline among the troops.

Then the colonies wisely decided that it was useless to attempt to choke the fountain of all their miseries except at its head. An address was sent to Queen Anne praying for help in the conquest of Nova Scotia and Canada, which was favourably received; and for the first time operations were concerted for a joint attack of imperial and colonial troops upon the French in North America. England was to supply a fleet and five regiments of the regular Army, Massachusetts and Rhode Island were to furnish twelve hundred men more, and these forces united were to attempt Quebec; while fifteen hundred men-from the other colonies, except from New Jersey and Pennsylvania, which selfishly kept apart, were to advance upon Montreal by Lake Champlain.

The troops of Massachusetts were mustered and drilled by British officers sent across the Atlantic for the purpose, and all signs pointed to a great and decisive effort. In due time the western contingent advanced towards Lake Champlain, by way of Albany and the Hudson, building on their way a fort at the carrying-place from the Hudson, which we shall know better as Fort Edward, and a second fort at Wood Creek, where the journey by water to Lake George was re-commenced, called Fort Anne. There the little column halted, for the brunt of the work was to fall on the fleet which was expected from England. The weeks flew on, but the fleet never appeared. The disaster of Almanza had upset all calculations and disconcerted all arrange-ments; and the great enterprise was perforce abandoned.

In July of the following year, however, an expedition on a smaller scale met with more success. A joint fleet of the Royal Navy and of colonial vessels, together with four regiments from New England and one of British marines, sailed against Port Royal, captured it after a trifling resistance, and changed its name to that which it still bears, of Annapolis Royal. Nova Scotia had changed hands many times, but from henceforth it was to remain British. Thus for the first time a British armament interposed seriously in the long strife between French and English in America. It was the beginning of the end, and of the end of more than French rule over the continent. A French of-ficer wrote at the time:

> If the French colonies should fall, Old England will not im-agine that these various provinces will then unite, shake off the yoke of the English monarchy, and erect themselves into a democracy.[11]

The idea of the capture of Canada, however, took root just at this time in the new English Ministry, where Bolingbroke and Harley had succeeded in ousting Marlborough from office. The conquest of New France would, they conceived, be a fine exploit to set off against the victories of the great duke. Massachusetts seconded the project with extraordinary zeal, and in July 1711 a British fleet with seven regular regiments on board sailed into Boston harbour. The disastrous issue of this enterprise has already been told. Bad seamanship cast eight of the transports on the rocks in the St. Lawrence, and seven hundred soldiers were drowned. General Hill and Admiral Walker were not the men to persist in the face of such a mishap, and the whole design was abandoned with disgraceful alacrity. The expedition was in fact simply a political move, conceived by factious politicians for factious ends instead of by military men for the benefit of the country, and accord-

11. Quoted by Parkman. *Half a Century of Conflict*, vol. i.

ingly it fared as such expeditions must inevitably fare.

Finally came the Peace of Utrecht, which gave England permanent possession of Newfoundland and of Acadia, though still without settlement of the vexed question as to the boundaries of the ceded province. These acquisitions entailed an increase of the British garrisons in America, as has already been told; but the entire strength of the British regular troops in New York, Nova Scotia, and Newfoundland did not exceed nine hundred men. The French, for their part, after the loss of Acadia betook themselves to Cape Breton, or, as they called it, L'Ile Royale, and set themselves forthwith to establish in one of the harbours a post which should command the access to Canada, and form a base for future aggression against New England and Nova Scotia.

A haven, named Port à l'Anglais, on the east coast was selected, and there was built the fort of Louisburg, the strongest on the Atlantic coast, and as the French loved to call it, the Dunkirk of America. The establishment of this fortress was one of those costly follies to which the French are prone, when failure and defeat allow them no outlet for their vexation and their spite. The climate absolutely forbade the construction of an elaborate stronghold of masonry. Fog and rain prevented mortar from setting all through the short spring and summer, fog and frost split mortar and stones and demolished walls every winter. Repairs were endless, yet the fortress was never in good repair, and the expense was intolerable. Lastly, such a stronghold was worthless without supremacy at sea.

But the French did not stop here. They lost no opportunity of stirring up the Acadians to discontent and of inflaming the Indians against the British both in Acadia and in New England. The result was a series of raids on the Kennebec, where the French, in order to guard the line of advance on Quebec by that river and Lake Chaudière, had established a chain of mission-stations. The colonists, goaded to exasperation, at last rooted out these missions by force, though not until after long delay owing to the perversity of the Assembly of Massachusetts, which, always jealous of the English governor, wished to take the control of operations out of his hand into their own, never doubting that their rustic ignorance would be as efficient as the tried skill of one of Marlborough's veterans.

So this state of outward peace and of covert war continued. France, despite the concessions made at the Peace of Utrecht, still claimed the whole of the North American continent, with some few trifling exceptions, and took every measure to make good her claim. A new

19

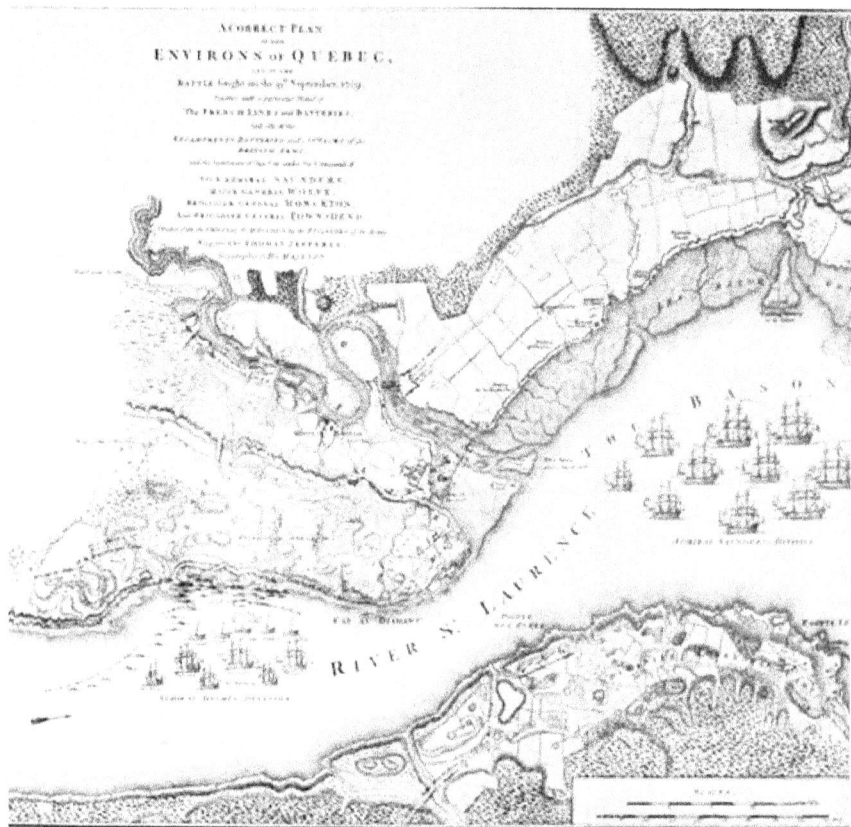

THOMAS JEFFREY'S

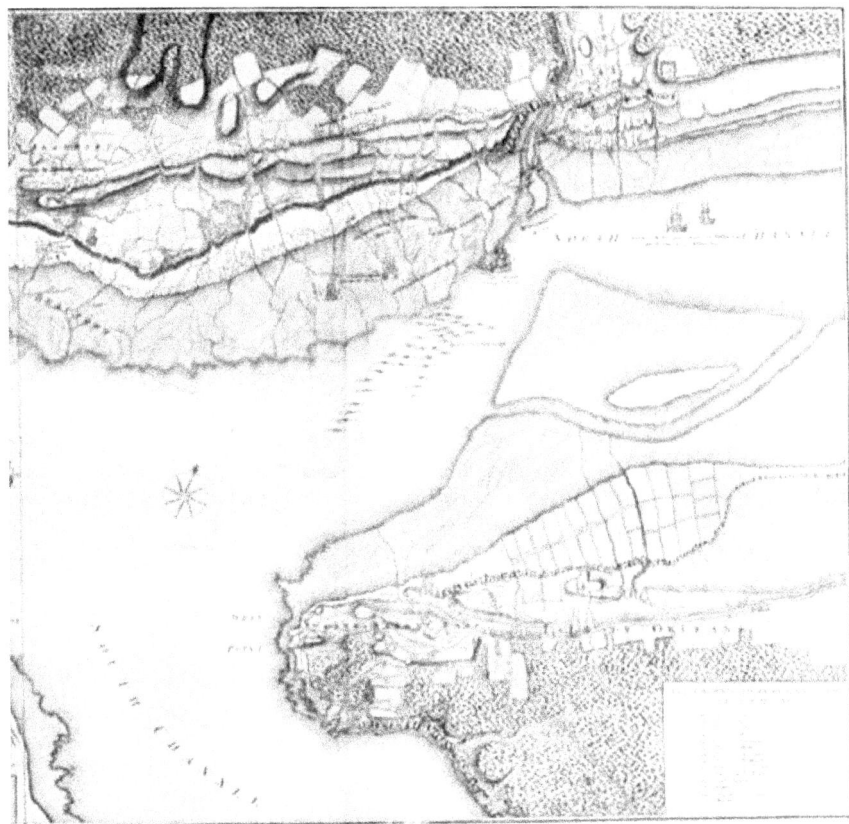

PLAN OF QUEBEC IN 1759

fort was erected at Niagara; another fort was built at Chambly to cover Montreal from any English attack by way of Lake Champlain, and in 1731 a massive stronghold of masonry was constructed at Crown Point, on the western shore of the same lake, and christened Fort Frederic. The ground on which this last fort stood was within the bounds claimed by New York, but the province was too busy over quarrels with her neighbour, New Jersey, to interpose.

So although New York and New England alike denounced the encroachment furiously, neither the one nor the other would lift a finger to prevent it. The one movement made by the colonists in counterpoise to the ceaseless activity of the French was the establishment of a fortified trading station at Oswego on Lake Ontario, as a rival to the French post at Niagara. Even this work was done not by the colonists but by Governor Burnet of New York at his own expense; and the debt due to him from the province on this account has never been liquidated to this day.

PART OF LAKE ONTARIO

PLAN of FORT NIAGARA,
with its ENVIRON.
Explanation.

A. The Fort.
B. The Dock & Harbour.
C. Two Lime Kilns.
D. The Brick Kiln.
E. The Burying Place.
F. The Approaches.
G. The First Battery.
H. The Second Battery.
I. The Third Battery.

Scale
200 Fathoms to an Inch.

T H E

R I V E R

Chapter 2

First Steps of Conflict

Thus matters drifted on in America until the war of the Austrian Succession. Then, as usual, the French at Louisburg received warning of the outbreak before the English at Boston, and the imperial garrisons at Annapolis Royal and at Canseau were overpowered and captured by the French without an effort. But now the colonists with superb audacity resolved to take the bull by the horns and to attack the French in the most formidable of their strongholds, Louisburg itself. The moving spirit in the enterprise was Governor William Shirley of Massachusetts, an Englishman by nationality and a barrister by training, who thought himself a born strategist; and the commander whom he selected was one William Pepperrell, a prosperous merchant of New England, whose father had emigrated as a poor man from his native Devon and had made his fortune.

Pepperrell had neither education nor experience in military matters, but he had shrewd good sense; while, being popular, he was likely to command the respect and obedience of his undisciplined troops. After some trouble the Provincial Assemblies were coaxed into approval of the design; four thousand men were raised in New England, a small fleet of armed vessels was collected for the protection of the transports, and the little expedition sailed to its rendezvous at Canseau, some fifty miles from Louisburg. Here by good luck it was joined by a British squadron under Commodore Warren, which threw in its lot with it; and the army of amateurs with its escort of hardy seamen proceeded with a light heart to the siege of the Dunkirk of America. The account of the operations is laughable in the extreme, though the French found them no matter for laughter. Skilled engineers the besiegers had none, and few if any skilled artillerymen, but they went to work with the best of spirits and good humour in their own casual fashion, which puzzled the French far more than a regular siege in form.

To be brief, with the help of gunners from the fleet and of extraordinary good fortune they succeeded in capturing the fortress after a siege of six weeks. The performance is certainly one of the curiosities of military history, but must be passed over in this place since it forms no part of the story of the British Army. [1] The colonists were not a little proud of the feat, and with right good reason. Nor did their gallant efforts pass without recognition in England. Pepperrell, who had amply justified Shirley's choice, was created a baronet; and on Warren's suggestion [2] the remains of the colonial troops were taken into English pay and formed into two regiments, with Pepperrell and Shirley for their colonels.

Though the colonial garrison suffered terribly from pestilence during the ensuing winter, [3] Shirley was anxious to complete the conquest of Canada in 1746; and Newcastle received his proposals with encouragement at Whitehall. Three British regiments—the Twenty-Ninth, Thirtieth, and Forty-Fifth—arrived in April to occupy Louisburg, and Newcastle promised five battalions more under Lieutenant-General St. Clair, together with a fleet under Warren, to aid in the operations. It was agreed that the British and the levies of New England should sail up the St. Lawrence to attack Quebec, while the remainder should, as usual, march against Montreal by way of Lake Champlain. The colonists took up the enterprise with great spirit, and the Provincial Assemblies of seven colonies voted a total force of forty-three hundred men. The French in Canada took the alarm and made frantic preparations for defence; but though the colonists were ready and eager at the time appointed, the British troops never appeared; Newcastle having detained them in Europe for the ridiculous descent upon L'Orient.

Shirley, undismayed, then decided to turn his little force against Crown Point; when all New England was alarmed by intelligence of a vast French armament on its way to retake Louisburg, recapture Acadia and burn Boston. Then the colonists took fright in their turn and equipped themselves for defence with desperate energy; but once again there was no occasion for panic. The French fleet sailed indeed, but after a voyage of disasters reached the coast of Nova Scotia only

---

1. The narrative, told with admirable vividness and humour, may be found in Parkman. *Half a Century of Conflict*, vol. ii.
2. Warren's letter, 4th July 1745.
3. 900 men were buried out of 2500.

A VIEW OF LOUISBURG, 1758

to be shattered and dispersed by a terrible storm. The commander-in-chief died of a broken heart, his successor threw himself on his own sword in despair, and after some weeks of helpless lingering in the harbour which now bears the name of Halifax, the fragments of the French fleet returned almost in a state of starvation to France.

Not discouraged by this terrible reverse the French Government in the following year sent out a second fleet, which was met off Rochelle by a superior fleet under Admirals Anson and Warren and utterly defeated. It was fortunate, for the British Government with Newcastle at its head gave the Americans no further help. Three hundred soldiers were indeed shipped off to Annapolis, but more than half of them died on the voyage, and many of the remainder, being gaol-birds and Irish papists, deserted to the French. The situation in Acadia was perilous, for the French population did not love their new masters, and the Canadians, particularly the Jesuit priests, never ceased to stimulate them to revolt. Shirley resolved that, though the security of Acadia was the charge of the mother country, the colonists must protect the province for themselves sooner than abandon it.

Massachusetts responded to his appeal with her usual spirit, and notwithstanding one severe reverse of the colonial troops, Acadia was still safe at the close of the war. For the rest, the French pursued their old method of hounding on the Indians against the British; and petty but barbarous warfare never ceased on the borders. For once, too, this warfare produced, though indirectly, an important result, since it brought to the front a young Irishman named William Johnson who, having shown an extraordinary power and ascendency over the Indians, was chosen as agent for New York in all dealings of the British with them. We shall see more of this Johnson in the years before us. Finally came the Peace of Aix-la-Chapelle, when the Americans to their huge disgust learned that Louisburg, their own prize, had been restored to France—bartered away for the retention of an insignificant factory upon the Indian sub-continent, called Madras.

The conclusion of the Peace of Aix-la-Chapelle was followed by the usual reduction of the forces in Britain. The ten new regiments and several other corps were disbanded, leaving for the cavalry all the regiments now in the Army List down to the Fourteenth Hussars, and in the infantry the Foot Guards and the First to the Forty-Ninth Regiments of the Line. The strength of all corps was of course diminished and the British Establishment was fixed at thirty thousand men, two-thirds of them for service at home and one-third for colonial garrisons. The rest of the army, thirty-seven regiments in all, but very weak in numbers, was as usual turned over to the Irish Establishment.

Efforts were of course made in both Houses of Parliament to cut down the numbers of the army to a still lower figure, and the antiquated arguments in favour of such a step were repeated as though they had not already done duty a thousand times within the past forty years. Nay, so vigorous is the old age of folly and of faction that men were still found, when the Mutiny Act was brought forward, to urge the needlessness of courts-martial in time of peace. These childish representations, however, received little notice or encouragement; while, on the other hand, divers projects for reform in the Army were brought forward which, even though they led to no result, received at least careful attention and intelligent debate. Of these matters it will be more convenient to speak when the narrative of the war is concluded. For although peace had been proclaimed, and estimates and establishment had been accordingly reduced, the struggle with France, far from being closed, was not even suspended abroad. It would seem that not a few members of both Houses were alive to the fact; while fugitive notices in the newspapers, announcing that "Mr. Clive, a volunteer, had the command given to him to attack a place called Arcourt," may have suggested it even to the gossips of the coffee-houses.

The government, however, was not one which could be expected to take thought for the morrow, or indeed for anything beyond the retention of power. It was that administration which had been formed by Henry Pelham in 1744, and is generally identified with the name of his brother, the Duke of Newcastle, who is remembered chiefly through his ignorance of the fact that Cape Breton is an island. This deplorable person possessed no talent beyond an infinite capacity for such intrigue as lifts incompetence to high office, and was only less of a curse to England than Madame de Pompadour was to France. One able man, however, there was in the lower ranks of the administration, William Pitt, who, after a vain effort to become Secretary at War, had accepted the post of Paymaster of the Forces. He now lay quiet, though not without occasional outbursts of mutiny, abiding his time and fulfilling the duties of his place with an integrity heretofore unknown in the Paymaster's Office.

One important military measure, meanwhile, the government did take. The number of men disbanded from fleet and army was so large that it was deemed prudent, in the interests alike of humanity and of public security, to make some provision for them. Accordingly fifty acres of freehold land, with an additional ten acres for every child, were offered to all veterans who would emigrate as settlers to Nova Scotia; their passage outward being likewise paid, and immunity from taxation guaranteed to them for ten years. The system was copied from the model given by the French in Canada, and by them doubtless borrowed from ancient Rome; but it was successful. Four thousand persons, with their families, took advantage of the offer, embarked under the command of Colonel Cornwallis and landed at the harbour of Chebucto, from thenceforward called, in honour of the President of the Board of Trade and Plantations, by the name of Halifax. Three companies of rangers were formed for the defence of the settlement, in addition to which two battalions of regular troops were detailed for the garrisons of Nova Scotia and Newfoundland. For it was intended that Halifax should be not only a refuge for disbanded soldiers, but a fortified station in counterpoise to the French fortress at Louisburg.

The French in Canada instantly took the alarm, and after their unscrupulous manner incited the Indians to murder the settlers, sparing no pains meanwhile to alienate the hearts of the Acadians from the British. The priests were their instruments in this treacherous policy, and their proceedings were fully approved at Versailles. What was called an Indian war was, in the plain words of Governor Hopson of Nova Scotia, no other than a pretence for the French to commit hostilities on British subjects. Yet through the trying years that followed, the British officials behaved always with exemplary patience and forbearance, though, owing to the incessant intrigues of the French, occasional skirmishes between French and English were unavoidable.

But British settlers had touched French America elsewhere on a more tender point even than in Acadia. British traders had found their way across the Alleghanies to the Ohio, and had stolen the hearts of the Indians on the river from their French rivals. To Canada this was a serious matter, for the chain of French posts that was designed to shut off the British from the interior ran from the Gulf of St. Lawrence to the Gulf of Mexico, and if the British should sever this chain at the Ohio French America would be parted in twain. In 1749 a French emissary was despatched from Montreal to vindicate French rights on the river and to bid the English traders depart from it.

His reception by the Indians was not encouraging, and even while he was on the spot a company was formed by some capitalists in Virginia to settle the country about the Ohio. The Governors of Pennsylvania and Virginia quickly perceived the importance of the position on the fork of the river where Pittsburg now stands, and were anxious to secure it by a fortified station; but unfortunately the public spirit of the colonies was less intelligent than the private enterprise. The Provincial Assemblies quarrelled with their governors and with each other, and refused to vote a farthing either for building a fort or for presents to conciliate the Indians in the valley of the Ohio.

Then, as usual, while the colonies debated and postponed the French took prompt and decisive action.

CHAPTER 3

Washington & the Ohio

In the summer of 1752 a new governor, Duquêsne, had arrived in Canada, who, as soon as the spring of 1753 was come, sent an expedition of fifteen hundred men through Lake Ontario to Lake Erie, where they landed on the eastern shore and built a fort of logs at Presquile, the site of the present Erie. Thence cutting a road for several leagues southward to French Creek (then called Rivière aux Bœufs), they constructed there a second fort named Fort le Bœuf, from which, when the water was high, they could launch their canoes on the creek and follow the stream downward to the Alleghany and the Ohio. The expedition was to have built a third fort at the junction of French Creek and the Alleghany, and descended the Ohio in order to intimidate the Indians, but the project was defeated by the sickliness of the troops. Garrisons were therefore left at Fort le Bœuf and Presquile, and the remainder of the force returned to Montreal, having thus secured communications between the St. Lawrence and the Ohio.

Governor Dinwiddie of Virginia no sooner heard of this movement on the part of the French than he sent a summons to the commanders of the forts to withdraw forthwith from the King of England's territory. The bearer of the message was the adjutant-general of the Virginian militia, a young man of twenty-one with a great destiny before him, George Washington. There were two British trading stations on the Ohio, Venango, at the junction of French Creek and the Alleghany, and Logstown, some miles below the site of Pittsburg. On arriving at Venango, Washington found it converted into a French military station, the officers of which received him hospitably, but told him that they had orders to take possession of the Ohio, and that "by God they would do it."

Making his way from thence to Fort le Bœuf, Washington delivered Dinwiddie's letter, and returned with the reply that it should be forwarded to Montreal, but that the garrisons had no intention of moving until orders should arrive from thence. Dinwiddie meanwhile had again appealed to the Virginian Assembly to vote money to build forts on the Ohio. He could show a letter from the Board of Ordnance in England approving of the project and offering arms and ammunition, as well as a letter from the king authorising the execution of the work at the colony's expense and the repelling of force by force; but the Assembly, though alive to the danger, would not vote a sixpence.

Such obstinacy was enough to drive a governor to despair, but Dinwiddie was blessed with considerable tenacity of purpose. A renewal of his appeal in the ensuing session was more successful, and the Assembly grudgingly voted a small and insufficient sum, with which the governor was forced to be content. Urgent applications to the neighbouring colonies for aid met with little response. The remoter provinces thought themselves in no way concerned; those nearer at hand refused help chiefly because their governors asked for it. It was in fact a principle with the Provincial Assemblies to thwart their governor, whether he were right or wrong, on every possible occasion; they being, as is so common in representative bodies, more anxious to assert their power and independence than their utility and good sense. North Carolina alone granted money enough for three or four hundred men.

However, the British Government had sanctioned the employment of the regular companies at New York and in Carolina, and Dinwiddie having raised three hundred men in Virginia, ordered them to the Ohio Company's station at Will's Creek, which was to be the base of operations. Meanwhile he despatched a party of backwoodsmen forthwith to the forks of the Ohio, there to build, on a site selected by Washington, the fort for which he had pleaded so long. Forty men were actually at work upon it when, on the 17th of April, a flotilla of small craft came pouring down on the Alleghany with a party of five hundred French on board.

The troops landed, trained cannon on the unfinished stockade, and summoned the British to surrender. Resistance was hopeless. The backwoodsmen perforce yielded; and the French having demolished their works erected a much larger and better fort on the same site, and called it Fort Duquêsne. The name before long was to be altered to Pittsburg, but the change was as yet hidden behind the veil of years.

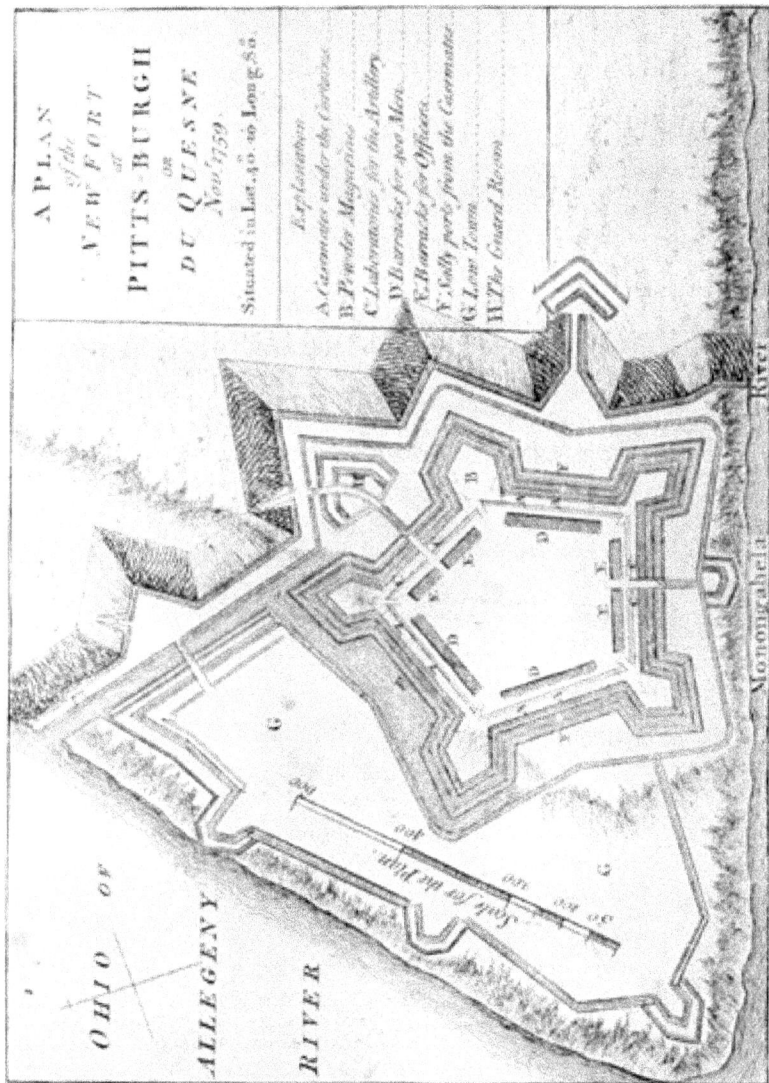

A PLAN
of the
NEW FORT
at
PITTS-BURGH
or
DU QUESNE
Nov 1759

Situated in Lat. 40.46 Long. 80.

Explanation

A Casemattes under the Curtains
B Powder Magazines
C Laboratory for the Artillery
W Barracks for 300 Men.
E Barracks for Officers.
F Sally ports from the Casemattes.
G Low Town.
W The Grated Room

OHIO or

ALLEGENY

RIVER

Scale for the Plan

Monongahela River

For the present the French had stolen a march on the British, and Dinwiddie was chagrined to the heart. He wrote:

If the Assembly had voted the money in November which they did in February, the fort would have been built and garrisoned before the French approached.

The governor, however, was by no means disposed meekly to accept this defeat. The French had expelled a British party from British territory by force of arms, and both he and Washington treated the incident as equivalent to a declaration of war. Washington, though but half of his troops had yet joined him, presently advanced over the Alleghanies to the Youghiogany, a tributary of the Monongahela; and there on the 27th of May he came upon a small party of French and fired the shots which began the war. A few weeks later he with his little force, something less than four hundred men, was surrounded by twice that number of Frenchmen, and after a fight of nine hours and the loss of a fourth of his men, was compelled to capitulate.

Dinwiddie was vexed beyond measure by this second reverse, and by the delay in the arrival of the reinforcements which had caused it. The two companies of regular troops from New York came crawling up to the scene of action in a disgraceful state. Their ranks were thin, for their muster-rolls had been falsified by means of "faggots"; they were undisciplined; they had neither tents, blankets, knapsacks, nor ammunition with them, nothing, in fact, but their arms and thirty women and children. [1]

The troops from North Carolina were still worse than these in the matter of discipline, so much so that they mutinied and dispersed to their homes while yet on the march to the rendezvous. The peril was great; yet the colonies remained supine. The Assembly of Virginia only after a bitter struggle granted Dinwiddie a competent sum; that of Pennsylvania, being composed chiefly of Quakers and of German settlers, who were anxious only to live in peace and to cultivate their farms, refused practically to contribute a farthing. New York was unable to understand, until Washington had been actually defeated, that there had been any French encroachment on British territory; Maryland produced a contribution only after long delay; and New Jersey, safely ensconced behind the shelter of her neighbours, flatly declined to give any aid whatever. New England alone, led as usual by Massachusetts, showed not only willingness but alacrity to drive back the

1. Holderness to Dinwiddie, 18th January 1754. Parkman, vol. i.

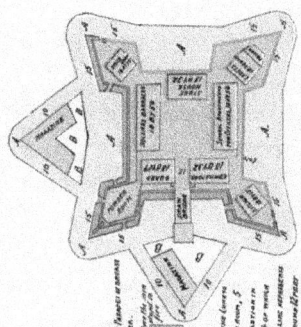

Nº 3

FORT DU QUESNE 1754.

Mills

MONONGAHELA

OHIO

ISLAND

Cornfield

BARK CABINS FOR THE SOLDIERS.

GARDENS

Corn field for ¾ of a Mile round.

Woods

A.A. Ditch with a breastwork
Towers up.
B. The earth dug out sent to the center.
C. The entrance of the French fort, S.
Cannon mounted on the bastion is
the whole fort, 8 Cannon & of which
three pounders. The principal members
Posts of wood driven in the ground & fixed
with a mortised treatise, with loop holes
for small arms.

detested French.

United action was as yet inconceivable by the colonists or, as the English more correctly called them, the Provincials. It was only in deference to representations from the British Government that New York, Pennsylvania, Maryland, and the four colonies of New England met in congress to concert for joint action in securing the unstable affections of the Indians. A project for colonial union broached by Benjamin Franklin at this same congress was wrecked by the jealousy of Crown and Colonies as to mutual concession of power.

In such circumstances the only hope lay in assistance from the mother country; and Dinwiddie accordingly sent repeated entreaties to England for stores, ammunition, and two regiments of regular infantry. The ministry at home was not of a kind to cope with a great crisis. Henry Pelham was dead; and the ridiculous Newcastle as Prime Minister had succeeded in finding a fool still greater than himself, Sir T. Robinson, to be Secretary of State in charge of the colonies. Nevertheless, in July ten thousand pounds in specie and two thousand stand of arms were shipped for the service of the colonies, [2] and on the 30th of September orders were issued for the Forty-Fourth and Forty-Eighth regiments, both of them on the Irish Establishment, to be embarked at Cork.

Each of these regiments was appointed to consist of three hundred and forty men only, and to take with it seven hundred stand of arms, so as to make up its numbers with American recruits. [3]

But the nucleus of British soldiers was presently increased to five hundred men, the augmentation being effected, as usual, by drafts from other regiments; not, however, without difficulty, for the service was unpopular, and there was consequently much desertion. The next step was to appoint a commander; and the choice fell upon General Edward Braddock, sometime of the Coldstream Guards. He was a man of the same stamp as Hawley, and therefore after the Duke of Cumberland's own heart, an officer of forty-five years' service, rough, brutal, [4] and insolent, a martinet of the narrowest type, but wanting neither spirit nor ability, and brave as a lion. His instructions were sufficiently wide, comprehending operations against the French in four

---

2. Holderness to Dinwiddie, 5th July 1754.

3. Order of 30th September 1754. *Record Office, America and W. I.,* vol. lxxiv.

4. Horace Walpole's instances of Braddock's rough manners are well known, but the following, I think, is new. An officer had been foisted upon Braddock on his appointment to the command, whom (in order to be rid of him), (cont. next page),

different quarters.

The French were to be driven from the Ohio, and a garrison was to be left to hold the country when captured; the like was to be done at Niagara, at Crown Point, and at Fort Beauséjour, a work erected by the French on the isthmus that joins Nova Scotia to the Continent. This plan had been suggested by Governor Shirley of Massachusetts; and in furtherance thereof the British Government had ordered two regiments, each one thousand strong, to be raised in America under the colonelcy of the veterans Shirley and Pepperrell, and to be taken into the pay of Great Britain. [5] There might well be doubt whether the means provided would suffice for the execution of the scheme.

It was January 1755 before the Forty-Fourth and Forty-Eighth were embarked at Cork, and past the middle of March before the whole of the transports arrived in Hampton Roads. Good care seems to have been taken of the troops on the voyage, for Braddock was able to report that there was not a sick man among them. [6] The transports were ordered to ascend the Potomac to Alexandria, where a camp was to be formed; and there on the 14th of April several of the governors met Braddock in council to decide as to the distribution of the work that lay before them. All was soon settled. Braddock with the two newly arrived regiments was to advance on Fort Duquêsne; Shirley with his own and Pepperrell's regiments was to attack Niagara; William Johnson, on account of his influence with the Indians, was chosen to lead a body of Provincial troops from New England, New Jersey, and New York against Crown Point; and to Lieutenant Colonel Monckton, an officer of whom we shall hear more, was entrusted the task of overpowering Fort Beauséjour.

The first and second of these operations were designed to cut the chain of French posts between the St. Lawrence and the Ohio, and may be described as purely offensive. Why, however, it should have been thought necessary to sever this chain at two points when one point would have sufficed, and why therefore the whole strength of the blow was not aimed at Niagara, are questions not easily to be

he placed in command of a small provincial fort at Cape Fear. Governor Dobbs of Carolina having complained of this officer, Braddock replied "that the man had been imposed upon him, that he would not trust him with the building of a hog-sty, and that the best thing Dobbs could do would be to hang him on the first tree he could find." The story is told in a letter of Governor Dobbs to General Amherst of 28th August 1762. *Record Office, W.O., Original Correspondence*, vol. xiii.
5. These, while they lasted, ranked as 51st and 52nd of the Line.
6. Braddock to Robinson, 18th March 1755.

Braddock's Route.
A.D. 1755.

answered. The capture of Crown Point would serve alike to bar a French advance southward at Lake Champlain and to further a British advance on Montreal, and hence combined objects both offensive and defensive. The reduction of Fort Beauséjour having no other purpose than the security of Acadia, was a measure wholly defensive.

The council broke up; the commanders repaired to their several charges, and Braddock was left to cope with his task. A great initial blunder had been made by the military authorities in England in sending the troops to Virginia and ordering them to advance on the Ohio by the circuitous route from Wills' Creek. This was, it is true, the line that had been taken by Washington; but Washington, like Shirley, was but an amateur, and a sounder military judgment would have shown that the suggestions of both were faulty. Disembarkation at Philadelphia, and a march directly westward from thence, would have saved not only distance and time but much trouble and expense; for Pennsylvania, unlike Maryland and Virginia, was a country rich in forage and in the means of transport.

CHAPTER 4

The Warpath

It was the collection of transport that was Braddock's first great difficulty. The Pennsylvanians showed an apathy and unwillingness which provoked even Washington to the remark that they ought to be chastised. It was only by the mediation of Benjamin Franklin, of all persons, that Braddock at last obtained waggons and horses sufficient for his needs. The general's trials were doubtless great, but his domineering temper, and the insolent superiority which he affected as an Englishman over Americans and as a regular officer over colonial militiamen, could not tend to ease the general friction between British and Provincials. His example was doubtless followed by his officers, the more so since it had been ordained that the king's commission should confer superiority in all grades, and that Provincial field-officers and generals were to enjoy no rank with Imperial officers of the same standing. Nevertheless Braddock was too capable a man to blind himself to the merit of the ablest of his coadjutors; and it was in terms honourable to himself that he invited and obtained the services of Colonel George Washington upon his staff.[1]

On the 10th of May Braddock reached his base at the junction of Wills' Creek with the Potomac, where the former trading station had been supplanted by a fort built of logs and called, in honour of the commander-in-chief, by the name of Fort Cumberland. It was a mere clearing in a vast forest, an oasis, as it has happily been termed, in a wilderness of leaves. [2] Here the troops had already been assembled, the Forty-Fourth and Forty-Eighth, each now raised by recruits

---

1. *Washington's Early Campaigns*, the French Post Expedition, Great Meadows and Braddock's Defeat—including Braddock's Orderly Books, by James Hadden is also published by Leonaur
2. Parkman.

40

from Virginia to a strength of seven hundred men, a detachment of one hundred of the Royal Artillery, thirty sailors lent by Commodore Keppel, helpful men as are all of their kind, and four hundred and fifty Virginian militia, excellently fitted for the work before them but much despised by the regular troops.

The whole force amounted to about twenty-two hundred men. Fifty Indian warriors, a source of unfailing interest to the bucolic British soldiers, were also seen in the camp in all their barbaric finery of paint and feathers; for Braddock, whatever his bigotry in favour of pipe-clay, was far too wise to underrate the value of Indian scouts.

A long month of delay followed, for the cannon did not arrive until a week later than Braddock, and the arrangements were still backward and confused. The general, doubtless with good reason, railed furiously at the roguery and ill-faith of the contractors; but it is sufficiently evident that what was lacking at headquarters was a talent for organisation. And meanwhile, though Braddock knew it not, events of incalculable moment were going forward elsewhere during those very weeks. The French had not failed to take note of the reinforcements sent by England to America, and had replied by equipping a fleet of eighteen ships and embarking three thousand troops to sail under their convoy to Canada.

The departure of this fleet was long delayed, and the dilatory British Government had time to despatch two squadrons to intercept it; but the French, putting to sea at last in May, contrived to elude the British cruisers and arrived safely at Louisburg and Quebec. Three only of their ships, having lagged behind the rest, found themselves off Cape Race in the presence of Admiral Boscawen's squadron. The two nations were nominally at peace, but the fleets opened fire, and the engagement ended in the capture of two of the French ships. Whether Newcastle desired it or not, England by this act was irrevocably committed to war.

It was just three days after this action that Braddock's force moved out of Fort Cumberland for its tedious march through the forest. Three hundred axemen led the way to cut and clear the road, which being but twelve feet wide was filled with waggons, pack-horses and artillery, so that the troops were obliged to march in the forest on either hand. Scouts scoured the ground in advance and flanking parties were thrown out against surprise, for Braddock was no mere soldier of the parade-ground. The march was insufferably slow, the horses being weak from want of forage, and the column dragged its length wearily along, "moving always in dampness and shade," [3] through the gloomy interminable forest.

Who can reckon the moral effect wrought on the ignorant and superstitious minds of simple English lads by that dreary trail through the heart of the wilderness? Day after day they toiled on without sight of the sun, and night after night over the camp-fire the Provincials filled them with hideous tales of Indian ferocity and assured them, in heavy jest, that they would be beaten. [4] The Forty-Eighth had stood firm at Falkirk; but the Forty-Fourth had suffered heavily at Prestonpans, during the Rebellion of '45, and such preparation could be wholesome for no regiment. Eight days' march saw the column advanced but thirty miles on its way, many of the men sick and most of the horses worn out, with no prospect ahead but that of a worse road than ever. Then came a report that five hundred French were on their way to reinforce Fort Duquêsne; and by Washington's advice Braddock decided to leave the heavy baggage, together with a guard under Colonel Dunbar, to follow as best it could, and himself to push on with a body of chosen troops.

Twelve hundred men were accordingly selected, and with these and a convoy reduced to ten guns, thirty waggons, and several pack-horses, the advance was resumed. Still progress continued to be wonderfully slow. The traditions of Flanders were strong in Braddock, and by dint of halting, as Washington said, to level every molehill and to throw a bridge over every brook, he occupied four whole days in traversing the next twelve miles.

At length, on the 7th of July, the column reached the mouth of Turtle Creek, a stream which enters the Monongahela about eight miles from its junction with the Alleghany, or in other words from Fort Duquêsne. The direct way, though the shorter, lay through a difficult country and a dangerous defile, so Braddock resolved to ford the Monongahela, fetch a compass, and ford it once more, in order to reach his destination. The French meanwhile had received intelligence of his advance on the 5th, and were not a little alarmed. The force at the disposal of M. Contrecoeur, the commandant of Fort Duquêsne, consisted only of a few companies of regular troops, with a considerable body of Canadians and nearly nine hundred Indians.

He resolved, however, to send off a detachment under Captain

---

3. Parkman.

4. Shirley to Newcastle, 5th Nov. 1755. He assigns this as one of the causes of the subsequent disaster.

NO. 1.

SKETCH OF BATTLE FIELD OF THE 9TH OF JULY UPON THE MONONGAHELA, SEVEN MILES FROM FORT DU QUESNE, SHOWING DISPOSITION OF TROOPS WHEN THE ACTION BEGAN.

M GENERALS GUARD IN MAIN BODY UPON THE FLANKS OF THE CONVOY WITH CATTLE AND PACK HORSES BETWEEN THEM.

G- WAGONS WITH POWDER AND TOOLS.
H- REAR GUARD OF ADVANCED PARTY.
I- LIGHT HORSE LEADING THE CONVOY.
K- SAILORS AND PIONEERS WITH TOOLS ETC. CATTLE AND PACK HORSES.
L- THREE FIELD PIECES.

TURTLE CREEK

R. MONONGAHELA.

A- FRENCH AND INDIANS WHEN FIRST DISCOVERED
B- GUIDES AND SIX LIGHT HORSE
C- VANGUARD OF ADVANCED PARTY
D- ADVANCED PARTY COMMANDED BY LT. COL. GAGE.
E- WORKING PARTY COMMANDED BY Sr. JNo. ST. CLAIR D.Q.M.G.
F- TWO FIELD PIECES.

▨ BRITISH TROOPS
◇ FRENCH AND INDIANS
+ CANNON AND HOWITZERS
◇ WAGONS, CARTS AND TUMBRILS
i CATTLE AND PACK HORSES

O- FIELD PIECES IN REAR OF CONVOY
P- RIVER GUARDS.
Q- FLANK GUARDS.
R- A HOLLOW WAY
S- A HILL FROM WHICH THE INDIANS DID MOST OF THE EXECUTION.
T- FRAZIER'S HOUSE

BRADDOCK'S BATTLEFIELD, JULY 9, 1755 (1)

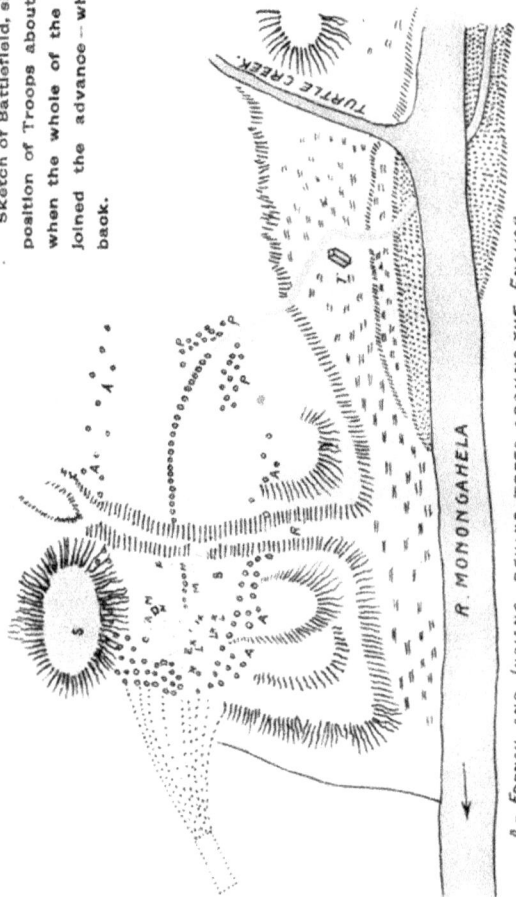

No. 2.

Sketch of Battlefield, showing disposition of Troops about 2 o'clock, when the whole of the main body joined the advance — when beaten back.

R. MONONGAHELA

TURTLE CREEK.

A = FRENCH AND INDIANS BEHIND TREES AROUND THE ENGLISH.
F = TWO FIELD PIECES OF THE ADVANCED PARTY ABANDONED.
C, D, E, H, K, M, N, O, = THE WHOLE BODY OF BRITISH JOINED WITH LITTLE OR NO ORDER, BUT ENDEAVORING TO MAKE FRONTS TOWARDS THE ENEMYS FIRE.
L = THE THREE FIELD PIECES OF THE MAIN BODY.
P = THE REAR GUARD DIVIDED BEHIND TREES.

BRADDOCK'S BATTLEFIELD, JULY 9, 1755 (2)

Beaujeu to meet the British on the march, and told off to that officer a force of about seventy regulars, twice as many Canadians, and six hundred and fifty Indians, or about nine hundred men in all. Early in the morning of the 8th this detachment marched away from Fort Du-quêsne, intending to wait in ambush for the British at some favourable spot, and by preference at the second ford of the Monongahela.

Braddock also had moved off early in the same morning, but it was nearly one o'clock when he forded the Monongahela for the second time. He himself fully expected to be attacked at this point, and had sent forward a strong advanced party under Lieutenant-Colonel Gage, to clear the opposite bank. No enemy however was encountered, for Beaujeu had been delayed by some trouble with his Indians, and had been unable to reach the ford in time. The main body of the British therefore crossed the river with perfect regularity and order, for Braddock wished to impress the minds of any Frenchmen that might be watching him with a sense of his superiority.

The sky was cloudless, and the men, full of confidence and spirit, took pride in a movement nearer akin than any other during their weary march to the displays of the parade-ground in which they had been trained. On reaching the farther bank the column made a short halt for rest, and then resumed the march along a narrow track parallel to the river and at the base of a steep ridge of hills. Around it on all sides the forest frowned thick and impenetrable; and Braddock took every possible precaution against surprise. Several guides, with six Virginian light horsemen, led the way; a musket-shot behind them came an advanced party of Gage's vanguard followed by the vanguard itself, and then in succession a party of axemen to clear the road, two guns with their ammunition-waggons, and a rear-guard. Then without any interval came the convoy, headed by a few light horsemen, a working party, and three guns; the waggons following as heretofore on the track, and the troops making their way through the forest to right and left, with abundance of parties pushed well out on either flank.

At a little distance from the ford the track passed over a wide and bushy ravine. Gage crossed this ravine with his advanced guard, and the main body was just descending to it when Gage's guides and horsemen suddenly fell back, and a man dressed like an Indian, but with an officer's gorget, was seen hurrying along the path. At sight of the British, Beaujeu (for the figure so strangely arrayed seems to have been no other) turned suddenly and waved his hat. The signal was followed by a wild war-whoop from his Indians and by a sharp fire upon the advancing British from the trees in their front. Gage's men at once deployed with great steadiness and returned the fire in a succession of deliberate volleys. They could not see a man of the enemy, so that they shot of necessity at haphazard, but the mere sound of the musketry was sufficient to scare Beaujeu's Canadians, who fled away shamefully to Fort Duquêsne. The third volley laid Beaujeu dead on the ground, and Gage's two field-pieces coming into action speedily drove the Indians away from the British front.

Meanwhile the red-coats steadily advanced, the men cheering lustily and shouting "God save the King"; and Captain Dumas, who had succeeded Beaujeu in the command of the French, almost gave up the day for lost. His handful of regular troops, however, stood firm, and he and his brother officers by desperate exertions succeeded in rallying the Indians. The regulars and such few of the Canadians as stood by them held their ground staunchly, and opened a fire of platoons which checked the ardour of Gage's men; while the Indians, yelling like demons but always invisible, streamed away through the forest along both flanks of the British, and there, from every coign of vantage that skilful bushmen could find, poured a deadly fire upon the hapless red-coats.

The cheering was silenced, for the men began to fall fast. For a time they kept their ranks and swept the unheeding forest with volley after volley, which touched no enemy through the trees. They could see no foe, and yet the bullets rained continually and pitilessly upon them from front, flank, and rear, like a shower from a cloudless sky. The trial at last was greater than they could bear. They abandoned their guns, they broke their ranks, and huddling themselves together like a herd of fallow-deer they fell back in disorder, a mere helpless mass of terrified men.

Just at this moment Braddock came up to the front. On hearing the fire he had left four hundred men under Colonel Sir Peter Halket of the Forty-Fourth to guard the baggage, and had advanced with the remainder to Gage's assistance. As the fresh troops came up, Gage's routed infantry plunged blindly in among them, seeking shelter from the eternal hail of bullets, and threw them likewise into confusion. In a short time the whole of Braddock's force, excepting the Virginians and Halket's baggage-guard, was broken up into a succession of heaving groups, without order and without cohesion, some facing this way, some facing that way, conscious only of the hideous whooping of the Indians, of bullets falling thickly among them from they knew not whence, and that they could neither charge nor return the fire.

The Virginians alone, who were accustomed to such work, kept their presence of mind, and taking shelter behind the trees began to answer the Indian fire in the Indian fashion. A few of the British strove to imitate them as well as their inexperience would permit; but Braddock would have none of such things. Such fighting was not prescribed in he drill-book nor familiar in the battlefields of Flanders, [5] and he would tolerate no such disregard of order and discipline. Raging and cursing furiously he drove British and Virginians alike back to their fellows with his sword; and then noting that the fire was hottest from a hill on the right flank of his advance, he ordered Lieutenant-Colonel Burton to attack it with the Forty-Eighth. The panic had already spread far, and it was only with infinite difficulty that Burton could persuade a hundred men to follow him. He was presently shot down, and at his fall the whole of his men turned back.

The scene now became appalling. The gunners stood for a time to their guns and sent round after round crashing uselessly into the forest; but the infantry stood packed together in abject terror, still loading and firing, now into the air, now into their comrades, or fighting furiously with the officers who strove to make them form. Braddock galloped to and fro through the fire, mounting fresh horses as fast as they were killed under him, and storming as though at a field-day. Washington, by miracle unwounded though his clothes were tattered with bullets, seconded him with as noble an example of courage and devotion; but it was too clear that the day was lost. Sixty out of eighty-six officers had fallen, and Braddock, after the slaughter had continued for three hours, ordered the wreck of his force to retreat.

He was still struggling to bring the men off in some kind of order when he fell from his horse, the fifth that the Indians' fire had compelled him to mount on that day, pierced by a bullet through arm and lungs. The unwounded remnant of his troops instantly broke loose and fled away. In vain Washington and others strove to rally them at the ford; they might as well have tried to stop the wild bears of the mountains. [6] They splashed through the river exhausted though they were, and ran on with the whoops of the Indians still ringing in their ears. Gage succeeded in rallying about eighty at the second ford; but

---

5. Compare the utter helplessness of the French at Wynendale, who made no effort to clear the woods on their flanks, and the confusion of the forest-fighting at Malplaquet.

6. Washington's own expression, in his letter of 18th July 1755.

the rest were not to be stayed.

Braddock, stricken to the death, begged to be left on the battle-field, but some officers lifted him and carried him away, for not a man of the soldiers would put a hand to him. Weak as he was, and racked with the pain of his wound and the anguish of his defeat, the gallant man still kept command and still gave his orders. On passing the Monongahela he bade his bearers halt, and sending Washington away to Dunbar for provisions and transport he passed the night among the handful of men that had been rallied by Gage.

On the next morning some order was restored, and the retreat was continued. Meanwhile stragglers had already reached Dunbar's camp with wild tidings of disaster and defeat, and many of the teamsters had already taken to their heels. After one more day of torture Braddock himself was carried into the camp.

On the march he had issued directions for the collection and relief of stragglers, and now he gave, or is said to have given, his last order, for the destruction of all waggons and stores that could not be carried back to Fort Cumberland. Accordingly scores of waggons were burned, the provisions were destroyed, and guns and ammunition, not easily to be replaced in the colonies, were blown up or spoiled. Then the relics of the army set out in shame and confusion for the return march of sixty miles to Fort Cumberland. Braddock travelled but a little distance with it. His faithful *aide-de-camp*, Captain Orme, though himself badly wounded, remained with him to the end and has recorded his last words; but there was little speech now left in the rough, bullying martinet, whose mouth had once been so full of oaths, and whose voice had been the terror of every soldier. It was not only that his lungs were shot through and through, but that his heart was broken. Throughout the first day's march he lay white and silent, with his life's blood bubbling up through his lips, nor was it till evening that his misery found vent in the almost feminine ejaculation, "Who would have thought it"? Again through the following day he remained silent, until towards sunset, as if to sum up repentance for past failure and good hope for the future, he murmured gently, "Another time we shall know better how to deal with them." And so having learned his lesson he lay still, and a few minutes later he was dead.

With all his faults this rude indomitable spirit appeals irresistibly to our sympathy. He had been chosen by the Duke of Cumberland, whose notions of an officer, in Horace Walpole's words, were drawn from the purest German classics, the classics initiated by Frederick

BRADDOCK'S DEFEAT

William and consecrated by Frederick the Great. It was the passion of the Hohenzollerns, great soldiers though they were, to dress their men like dolls and to manipulate them like puppets; but, dearly though they loved the mechanical exercise of the parade-ground, they knew that the minuteness of training and the severity of discipline thereby entailed were but means to an end.

In the eyes of Cumberland, though he was very far from a blind or a stupid man, powder, pipe-clay, and precision loomed so large as to appear an end in themselves. He could point too to the initial success of his attack at Fontenoy, which was simply an elaborate parade-movement; but he forgot that the battlefields of a Prussian army and the adversaries of a Prussian general were to be found on the familiar lands of Silesia, Brandenburg, and Saxony, whereas the fighting-grounds of the British were dispersed far and wide among distant and untrodden countries, and their enemies such as were not to be encountered according to the precepts of Montecuculi and Turenne. It was as a favourite exponent of Cumberland's military creed that Braddock was sent to North America. He was born and trained for such actions as Fontenoy; and it was his fate to be confronted with a difficult problem in savage warfare. His task was that which since his day has been repeatedly set to British officers, namely to improvise a new system of fighting wherewith to meet the peculiar tactics of a strange enemy in a strange country. Too narrow, too rigid, and too proud to apprehend the position, he applied the time-honoured methods of Flanders, and he failed.

Other officers have since fallen into the like error, owing not a little to a false system of training, and have failed likewise; and vast as is our experience in savage warfare, it may be that the tale of such officers is not yet fully told. Nevertheless, though Braddock's ideal of a British officer may have been mistaken, it cannot be called low. In rout and ruin and disgrace, with the hand of death gripping tightly at his throat, his stubborn resolution never wavered and his untameable spirit was never broken. He kept his head and did his work to the last, and thought of his duty while thought was left in him. His body was buried under the road, that the passage of the troops over it might obliterate his grave and save it from desecration from the Indians. But the lesson which he had learned too late was not lost on his successors, and it may truly be said that it was over the bones of Braddock that the British advanced again to the conquest of Canada.

The losses in this disastrous action were very heavy; the devotion of the officers, whose conduct was beyond all praise, leading them almost to annihilation. Among the wounded were two men who were to become conspicuous at a later day, Gage the leader of the advanced guard and Captain Horatio Gates of the garrison of New York. Of thirteen hundred and seventy-three non-commissioned officers and men, but four hundred and fifty-nine came off unharmed; and the wounded that were left on the field were tortured and murdered by the Indians after their barbarous manner. The loss of the French was trifling. Three officers were killed and four wounded, all of them at the critical moment while their men were wavering; nine white men also were killed and wounded, and a larger but inconsiderable number of Indians.

It was in fact a total and crushing defeat. Yet Count Dieskau, an officer high in the French service in Canada, expressed no surprise when he heard of it, for it was the French rule, founded on bitter experience, never to expose regular troops in the forest without a sufficient force of Indians and irregulars to cover them. The Virginians, whose admirable behaviour had been the one creditable feature in the action, had shown that abundance of good irregular troops were to be found in America; and it was evident that the British needed only to learn from their enemies in order to defeat them.

CHAPTER 5

First Operations

The first blow against the French in America had failed; it must now be seen how it fared with the operations entrusted to Shirley, Johnson, and Monckton. Shirley, at Massachusetts, had been busy since the beginning of the year in calling the Northern provinces to arms, and they had responded nobly, Massachusetts alone raising forty-five hundred men, and the rest of New England and New York nearly three thousand more. The point first selected for attack was Fort Beauséjour on the Acadian isthmus, for which object two thousand volunteers of New England were sent up to Monckton. Adding to them a handful of regular troops from the garrison, [1] Monckton sailed away without delay to his work.

On the 1st of June the expedition anchored in the bay before Fort Beauséjour, which after a fortnight's siege and the feeblest of defences fell, together with a smaller fort called Fort Gaspereau, into Monckton's hands. This success was followed by the expulsion of the greater part of the French population from Acadia, a harsh measure necessitated entirely by the duplicity of the Jesuit priests and of the Canadian Government, who had never ceased to stir up the unhappy peasants to revolt. From henceforth, therefore, Acadia may be dismissed from the sphere of active operations.

The attack on Crown Point was a more serious matter, for which the force entrusted to William Johnson included some three thousand Provincial troops from New England and New Hampshire, and hundred Indians. Johnson had seen no service and was innocent of all knowledge of war, but his influence with the Indians was very great, and as he came from New York his appointment could not but be

---

1. Probably of the 40th Foot, but possibly of the 45th.

MAJOR GENERAL ROBERT MONCKTON

pleasing to that province. His men were farmers and farmers' sons, excellent material but neither drilled nor trained. With the exception of one regiment, all wore their own clothes, and far the greater number brought with them their own arms. After long delay, owing to the jealousies of the various provinces and to defective organisation, the force was assembled at Albany, and in August began to move up the Hudson towards Lake George, a new name bestowed by Johnson in honour of his sovereign. At the carrying-place, where the line of advance left the Hudson, was built a fort, which was first called Fort Lyman but subsequently Fort Edward, by which latter name the reader should remember it. Here five hundred men were left to complete and to man the works, while the remainder, moving casually and leisurely forward, advanced to the lake and encamped upon its southern border.

Meanwhile the French, warned by papers captured from Braddock of the design against Crown Point, had sent thither thirty-five hundred regular troops, Canadians and Indians, under the command of Count Dieskau, an officer who had served formerly under Marshal Saxe. There were two lines by which Johnson could advance against them, the one directly up Lake George, the other by the stream named Wood Creek, which runs parallel with it into Lake Champlain. The junction of both passages is commanded by a promontory on the western side of Lake Champlain, called by the French Carillon, but more famous under its native name of Ticonderoga. To this point Dieskau advanced with a mixed force of fifteen hundred men, and from thence pushed forward to attack Johnson in his camp.

The sequel may be briefly told. Johnson had imprudently detached five hundred men with some vague idea of cutting off Dieskau's retreat; and these were caught in an ambuscade and very roughly handled. But when, elated by this success, Dieskau advanced against Johnson's camp he was met by a most stubborn resistance; and finally his troops were driven back in disorder and he himself wounded and taken prisoner. Johnson, however, did not follow up this fortunate success. Shirley repeatedly adjured him to advance to Ticonderoga, but was answered that the troops were unable to move through sickness, indiscipline, bad food, and bad clothing. Johnson lingered on in his camp until the end of November, with his men on the verge of mutiny, and having built a fort at the southern end of the lake, which he called Fort William Henry, retreated to the Hudson. He was rewarded for his victory by a vote of five thousand pounds from the British Parliament and by a baronetcy from the king; but none the less his enterprise was a fail-

Scale to this Plan of the Fort.

Fort

William

Henry.

A

B

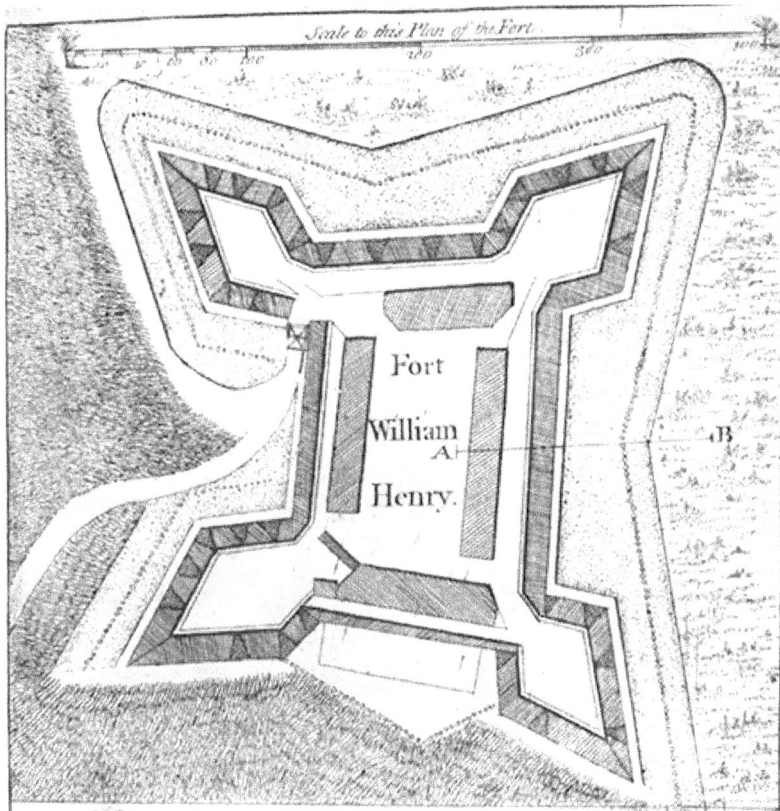

Section through A.B.

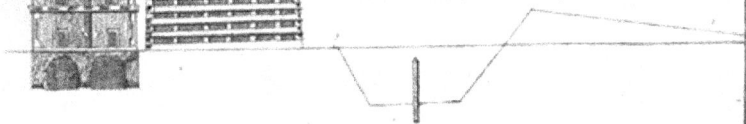

A Scale to the Profile

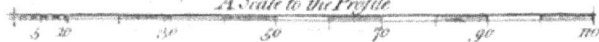

5 10   30   50   70   90   110

ure, and Crown Point was left safely in the hands of the French.

The expedition against Niagara was undertaken by Shirley himself, in all the pride of a lawyer turned general. Hitherto he had but planned campaigns on paper; now he was to execute one in the field. His base of operations was, like Johnson's, the town of Albany, and his force consisted of his own regiment and Pepperrell's, which, although the King's troops and wearing the king's uniform, consisted none the less of raw Provincial recruits, together with one regiment of New Jersey militia, in all twenty-five hundred men.

From Albany the force ascended the river Mohawk in bateaux to the great carrying-place, where the town of Rome now stands; from which point the *bateaux* were drawn overland on sledges to Wood Creek, [2] where they were again launched to float down stream to Lake Oneida and so to the little fort of Oswego on Lake Ontario. As might have been expected with an amateur, Shirley's force arrived at its destination long before his supplies, so that his force was compelled to wait for some time inactive and on short rations. The French, too, having learned of this design also from the papers taken at the Monongahela, had reinforced their garrisons not only at Niagara but at Fort Frontenac at the north-eastern outlet of the lake. This materially increased Shirley's difficulties, for unless he first captured Frontenac the French could slip across the lake directly he was fairly on his way to Niagara, take Oswego and cut him off from his base. To be brief, the task, rendered doubly arduous by dearth of provisions, was too great for Shirley's strength; and at the end of October he abandoned the enterprise, having accomplished no more than to throw a garrison of seven hundred men into Oswego.

So amid general disappointment ended the American campaign. Of the four expeditions one only had succeeded; all of the rest had failed, one of them with disaster. Nor did this disaster end with the retreat from the Monongahela, for no sooner had Dunbar retired from the frontier than the Indians, at the instigation of the French, swarmed into Virginia, Maryland, and Pennsylvania to the massacre and pillage of the scattered settlements on the border. Washington with fifteen hundred Virginian militia did what he could to protect three hundred miles of frontier, but with so small a force the duty was far beyond his power or the power of any man.

Reinforce him, however, the Assembly of Pennsylvania would not. They closed their ears even to the cry of their own settlers for arms

2. Not to be confounded with the Wood Creek on Lake Champlain.

and ammunition, and for legislation to enable them to organise themselves for defence. The Assembly was intent only on fighting with the Governor. The members would yield neither to his representations nor to the entreaties of their fellow-citizens; and it was not until the enemy had advanced within sixty miles of Philadelphia that, grudgingly and late, they armed the governor with powers to check the Indian invasion. It was none too soon, for the French had taken note of the large population of pauperised Germans, Irish, "white servants," and transported criminals in Pennsylvania, and were preparing to turn it into a recruiting-ground for the French service. [3]

Thus closed the year 1755, with hostilities in full play between English and French in North America. Yet war had not been declared, nor, though it was certain to come, had any preparation been made for it.

---

3. Intercepted letter in *Col. Papers* (America and West Indies), vol. lxxxi. March 1756

Chapter 6

The Broader Scene

The measures taken at the beginning of 1755 sufficiently indicate the feebleness and vacillation of a foolish and effete British Administration. In February some addition had been made to the infantry by raising the strength of the Guards and of seven regiments of the Line; and in March the king sent a message to Parliament requesting an augmentation of the forces by land and sea. The ministry employed the powers thus given to them in raising five thousand marines in fifty independent companies, and placing them expressly under the command of the Lord High Admiral.

It is said [1] that Newcastle refused to raise new regiments from jealousy of the Duke of Cumberland's nomination of officers, and there is nothing incredible in the assertion. But though this measure pointed at least to activity on the part of the fleet, never were British ships employed to less purpose. The squadron sent out under Boscawen to intercept the French reinforcements on their way to Louisburg was considerably inferior to the enemy's fleet, and required to be reinforced, of course at the cost of confusion and delay, before it was fit to fulfil its duty. Fresh trouble was caused in May by the king's departure for Hanover, a pleasure which he refused to deny himself despite the critical state of affairs in England.

During his absence his power was delegated, as was customary, to a Council of Regency, a body which was always disposed to reserve matters of importance for the king's decision, and was doubly infirm of purpose with such a creature as Newcastle among its ruling spirits. A powerful fleet under Sir Edward Hawke was ready for sea and for action; and the Duke of Cumberland, remembering the consequences

---

1. Walpole.

of peaceful hostility in 1742 and 1743, was for throwing off the mask, declaring open war and striking swiftly and at once. He was, however, overruled, and Hawke's fleet was sent to sea with instructions that bound it to a violation of peace and a travesty of war. The king meanwhile was solicitous above all things for the security of Hanover. Subsidiary treaties with Bavaria and Saxony for the protection of the Electorate had for some time existed, but were expired or expiring; and now that some return for the subsidies of bygone years seemed likely to be required, the contracting States stood out for better terms. The king therefore entered into a new treaty with Hesse-Cassel for the supply of eight thousand men, and with Russia for forty thousand more, in the event of the invasion of Hanover.

With these treaties in his pocket he returned to England, to find the nation full of alarm and discontent. Nor was the nation at fault in its feelings. In August the news of Braddock's defeat had arrived and had been received with impotent dismay. Yet nothing was done to retrieve the disaster, and two full months passed before a few thousand men were added to all three arms of the army. [2] Meanwhile Newcastle, after vainly endeavouring to persuade Pitt to serve under him, had strengthened his ministry somewhat by securing the accession of Henry Fox; and on the 13th of November the king opened Parliament, announcing, as well he might, the speedy approach of war. A long debate followed, wherein Pitt surpassed himself in denunciation of subsidiary treaties and contemptuous condemnation of Newcastle; but the party of the court was too strong for him, and the treaties were confirmed by a large majority. Pitt was dismissed from his office of Paymaster, and Fox having been promoted to be Secretary of State was succeeded by Lord Harrington as Secretary at War. Lastly, some weeks later, General Ligonier was most unjustly ousted from the post of Master-General of the Ordnance, to make way for a place-hunter who was not ashamed thus to disgrace his honoured title of Duke of Marlborough. It seemed, in fact, as though there were a general conspiracy to banish ability from high station.

A fortnight later the estimates for the army were submitted to Parliament. Notwithstanding the urgent danger of the situation, the number of men proposed on the British Establishment little exceeded thirty-four thousand men for Great Britain and thirteen thousand

---

2. Twenty battalions of the Line raised to a strength of a thousand men each; eleven regiments of cavalry augmented; two new companies added to the artillery. *Miscellaneous Orders*, October 1755. *Warrant Books*, 21st October 1755.

for the colonies. A few days afterwards the question was debated, and Barrington then announced a further increase of troops; whereupon Pitt very pertinently asked the unanswerable question why all these augmentations were made so late. The House, however, was in earnest as to the military deficiencies of the country. Fox had taunted Pitt by challenging him to bring forward a Militia Bill, and Pitt seized the opportunity offered by a debate on the Militia to give the outlines of a scheme for making that force more efficient. His proposals were embodied in a bill, which formed the basis of the Militia Act that was to be passed, as shall be seen, in the following year. So far therefore the Commons forced upon the government and the country at least the consideration of really valuable work.

On the re-assembly of Parliament after Christmas an estimate was presented for the formation of ten new regiments, to be made up in part of certain supplementary companies which had been added to existing battalions in 1755. These new regiments were, in order of seniority, Abercromby's, Napier's, Lambton's, Whitmore's, Campbell's, Perry's, Lord Charles Manner's, Arabin's, Anstruther's and Montagu's, and they are still with us, (1899), numbered in succession the Fiftieth to the Fifty-Ninth. [3] At the same time a new departure was made by adding a light troop apiece to eleven regiments of dragoons, both men and horses being specially equipped for the work which is now expected of all cavalry, but which was then entrusted chiefly to ir-regular horse formed upon the model of the Austrian Hussars. Yet another novelty was foreshadowed in February when a bill was intro-duced to enable the king to grant commissions to foreign Protestants in America.

The origin of this measure, according to Horace Walpole, was a proposal made by one Prevost, a Protestant refugee, to raise four bat-talions of Swiss and Provincials in America, with a British officer for colonel-in-chief but with a fair number of foreigners holding other commissions. Quite as probably this new step was quickened, if not suggested, by the news that the French contemplated the enlistment of recruits among the foreign population of British America. The vote for these four battalions was passed without a division, though Pitt opposed the bill with all his power and was supported by a petition from the Agent of Massachusetts. He was vehement for the employ-ment of British soldiers to fight British battles; whereas so far the most important military measure of king and ministers had been the

---

3. Order for raising them. *Miscellaneous Orders*, 7th January 1756.

hiring of Germans. The bill was none the less passed, and on the 4th of March the order for the enlistment of the four battalions was given. Lord Loudoun was to be their colonel-in-chief, Pennsylvania their recruiting-ground, and their title the Royal Americans, an appellation long since displaced by the famous number of the Sixtieth—senior regiment of green clad riflemen destined for fame under Wellington in the Iberian Peninsula.

Amid all these preparations, however, the nation throughout the first months of 1756 lived in abject terror of an invasion. France on her side had not been backward in equipping herself for the approaching contest. Great activity at Toulon had been followed by equal activity at Dunkirk, and despite good information as to the true object of the armaments fitted out at these two ports, the people naturally, and the government most culpably, persisted in the belief that they were designed for a descent upon Britain herself. Few troops were ready to meet such a descent, for votes cannot improvise trained officers and men, and the folly of the administration had done its worst to discourage enlistment.

When the danger seemed nearest, many great landowners had interested themselves personally and with great success to obtain recruits; and among others Lord Ilchester and Lord Digby in Somerset had attracted some of the best material to be found in rural England, promising that the men so enlisted should not be required to serve outside the kingdom. Notwithstanding this pledge, however, these recruits were by order of the ministry forcibly driven on board transports and shipped off to Gibraltar. Never was there more brutal and heartless instance of the ill-faith kept by a British Government towards the British soldier. Having thus checked the flow of recruits at home, the ministry turned to Holland and asked for the troops which she was bound by treaty to furnish. The request was refused; whereupon a royal message was actually sent to Parliament announcing that the king in the present peril had sent for his contingent of Hessian troops from Germany, for the defence of England.

The message was received with murmurs in the Commons, as well it might be, but it was not opposed; and indeed the climax of disgrace was not yet reached. Whether from desire to embarrass Newcastle or to pay court to the king, Lord George Sackville, an officer whom before long we shall know too well, expressed a preference for Hanoverians over Hessians, and proposed an address praying the king to bring over his own electoral troops. Pitt left his sickbed and came down, ill as he was, to the House, to appeal to the history of the past and to the pride of every Englishman against the motion; yet it was passed by a majority of nearly three to one. The Lords consented to join the Commons in this address, the king granted their prayer, and the result was that both Hanoverians and Hessians were imported to defend this poor Island that could not defend herself.

The next business brought before Parliament furnished new evidence of the general confusion of affairs. As might have been foreseen, Frederick of Prussia had viewed with no friendly eye the treaty made by King George with Russia; and he now proposed, as an alternative, that Hanover and England should combine with Prussia to keep all troops whatsoever from entering the German Empire. Since Frederick had already announced his intention of attacking the Russians if they moved across the frontier, and since there was good reason to apprehend that, if driven to desperation, he might join with the French in overrunning Hanover, the Russian treaty was thrown over, and the new arrangement accepted by King George.

The pecuniary conditions attached to the agreement were duly ratified by the House of Commons in May, with results that were to reach further than were yet dreamed of. Then at last, apparently as an after-thought, war was formally declared. The country being thus definitely committed to a struggle which might be for life or death, the Lords supported by Newcastle seized the opportunity to reject the Militia Bill, which was the one important military measure so far brought forward. The general helplessness of the moment, owing to the absence of a strong hand at the helm, is almost incredible.

Meanwhile the French had struck their first blow, not on the shores of Britain, but at Minorca. As early as in January the Ministry had received good intelligence of the true destination of the enemy's armaments, but had made no sufficient preparation to meet the danger; nor was it until the 7th of April that it sent a fleet of ten ships, ill -manned and ill-found, under Admiral Byng to the Mediterranean. On the day following Byng's departure twelve ships of the line under M. de la Galissonière, with transports containing sixteen thousand troops under the Duke of Richelieu, weighed from Toulon, and on the 18th dropped anchor off the port of Ciudadella, at the north-western end of Minorca. General Blakeney, the governor, had received warning of the intended attack two days before, and had made such preparations as he could for defence; but the means at his disposal were but poor. He had four regiments, the Fourth, Twenty-Third, Twenty-Fourth, and Thirty-Fourth of the Line; to which Commodore Edgcumbe, who was lying off Mahon with a squadron too weak to encounter the French, had added all the marines that he could spare before sailing away to Gibraltar.

Even so, however, Blakeney could muster little more than twenty-eight hundred men. But his most serious difficulty was lack of officers. He himself had won his ensigncy under Cutts the Salamander at Venloo, and he had maintained his reputation for firmness and courage at Stirling in 1745, but he was now past eighty, crippled with gout and unfit to bear the incessant labours of a siege. Nevertheless he was obliged to take the burden upon him from sheer dearth of senior officers. The lieutenant-governor of the island, the governor of its principal defence, Fort Philip, and the colonels of all four regiments were absent; nineteen subalterns had never yet joined their respective corps, and nine more officers were absent on recruiting duties. In all five-and-thirty officers were wanting at their posts. It was the old evil against which George the First had struggled in vain, and it was now about to bear bitter fruit.

Richelieu landed on the 18th, and Blakeney at once withdrew the whole of his force to Fort St. Philip in order to make his stand there. This fortress, which commanded the town and harbour of Mahon, was probably the most elaborate possessed by the British, and was inferior in strength to few strongholds in Europe. Apart from the ordinary elaborations of the school of Vauban, it was strengthened by countless mines and galleries hewn out of the solid rock, which afforded unusual protection to the defenders. Blakeney had little time to break up the roads or otherwise to hinder the French advance; and Richelieu, marching into the town of Mahon on the 19th, was able a few days later to begin the siege. His operations, however, were unskilfully conducted, and the garrison defended itself with great spirit.

An officer of engineers, Major Cunningham by name, while on his way to England from Minorca on leave, had heard of the French designs upon the island and had instantly hurried back to his old post to assist in the defence; and his skill and resource were of inestimable value. So clumsily in fact did the French manage their operations that it was not until the 8th of May that their batteries began to produce the slightest effect.

Byng meanwhile had arrived at Gibraltar and had learned what was going forward. He carried the Seventh Fusiliers on board his fleet for Minorca, and had orders to embark yet another battalion from

Gibraltar as a further reinforcement. General Fowke, however, who was in command at the Rock, urged that his instructions on this latter point were discretionary only and that he could not spare a battalion, having barely sufficient men to furnish reliefs for the ordinary guards. He therefore declined to grant more than two hundred and fifty men, to replace the marines landed from the fleet by Commodore Edgcumbe.

It is instructive to note the difficulties imposed upon the commanders by the neglect of the government. Hitherto one of the first measures taken in prospect of a war had been the reinforcement of the Mediterranean garrisons. Now, after a full year of warning, they were left unstrengthened and unsupported. Nay, Richelieu had lain in front of Fort St. Philip for three whole weeks before three battalions were at last ordered to sail for Gibraltar. [4]

Byng's fleet was so slenderly manned that he required the Seventh Fusiliers for duty on board ship, and therefore asked Fowke for a battalion for Minorca; Fowke's position was so weak that he dared not comply; and Blakeney's force was so inadequate that, though he could indeed hold his own in the fortress, he dared not venture his troops in a sortie. At length on the 19th of May Byng came in sight of Fort St. Philip, and on the following day fought the indecisive action and made the unfortunate retreat which became memorable through his subsequent fate. The besieged, though greatly disappointed by his withdrawal, still defended themselves stoutly and with fine spirit. The fortress was well stored and the batteries were well and effectively served. Six more battalions were now sent to Richelieu, and the French plan of attack was altered. New batteries were built, which on the 6th of June opened fire from over one hundred guns and mortars, inflicting much damage and making a considerable breach.

The British repaired the injured works and stood to their guns as steadily as ever; but on the 9th the French fire reopened more hotly than before and battered two new breaches. Matters were now growing serious; and on the 14th a party of the garrison made a sally, drove the French from several of their batteries and spiked the guns, but pursuing their success too far were surrounded and captured almost to a man. Still Richelieu hesitated to storm; nor was it until the night of the 27th that he nerved himself for a final effort and made a grand attack upon several quarters of the fortress simultaneously. The defence was of the stubbornest, and the successful explosion of a mine sent

4. The 53rd, 54th and 57th. *Secretary's Common Letter Book*, 12th May 1756.

three companies of French grenadiers flying into the air; but three of the principal outworks were carried, and the ablest officer of the garrison, Lieutenant Colonel Jefferies, while hurrying down to save one of them, was cut off and made prisoner with a hundred of his men.

Cunningham also was severely wounded and rendered unfit for duty. With hardly men enough left to him to man the guns, Blakeney on the 28th capitulated with the honours of war, and the garrison was embarked for Gibraltar. The siege had lasted for seventy days and had cost the French at the least two thousand men. The losses of the garrison were relatively small, amounting to less than four hundred killed and wounded, and the surrender was no dishonour to the British Army; but there was no disguising the disgraceful fact that Minorca was gone.

On the 14th of July the news reached England, and the nation, frantic with rage and shame, looked about savagely for a scapegoat. Bitter and cruel attacks were made even upon poor old Blakeney, who for all his fourscore years had never changed his clothes nor gone to bed during the ten weeks of the siege. Fowke was tried by court-martial for disobedience of orders in refusing to send the battalion required of him from Gibraltar, and though acquitted of all but an error in judgment and sentenced to a year's suspension only, was dismissed the service by the king. Finally, as is well known, the public indignation fastened itself upon Byng; and the unfortunate admiral was shot because Newcastle deserved to be hanged. Old Blakeney alone, as was his desert, became a hero and was rewarded with an Irish peerage. Amid all the disgrace of that miserable time men found leisure to chronicle with a sneer that the veteran went to court in a hackney coach with a foot-soldier behind it. St. James's would not have been the worse for a few more courtiers and lacqueys of the same rugged stamp.

More disasters were at hand; but the general paralysis in England continued. Such troops as the country possessed were still distributed as though an invasion were imminent. There was a camp at Cheltenham under Lord George Sackville, and another in Dorsetshire; the Hessians were at Winchester, the Hanoverians about Maidstone, the artillery massed together under the Duke of Marlborough at Byfleet; all doing nothing when there was so much to be done. The news of Braddock's defeat was nearly eight months old when Byng sailed for the Mediterranean, but not a man had been embarked to America.

CHAPTER 7

The Fall of Oswego

Up to the end of March, 1756, the only step taken had been the despatch of Colonel Webb to supersede Shirley as commander-in-chief, but with instructions to yield the command to General Abercromby, who was also under orders for America, on his arrival; while Abercromby in turn was to give place to Lord Loudoun. At last, towards the end of April the Thirty-Fifth Foot and the Forty-Second Highlanders were embarked and reached New York late in June; and a month later Lord Loudoun arrived and assumed the command. Pitt before its departure had described the force under Loudoun's orders as a scroll of paper, and the description was little remote from the truth. Of the Sixtieth hardly one battalion was yet raised; Shirley's and Pepperrell's regiments, or what was left of them, were in garrison at Oswego; and the levies of the various colonies as usual were long in enlisting, late in arriving, and not too well supplied. Finally, each several contingent was jealously kept by its province under its own orders and control.

Shirley, undismayed by the failures of the previous year, meditated further operations in the direction of Fort Frontenac and Niagara, and against Crown Point; and with this view he had accumulated supplies along the route to Oswego on the one hand, and at Forts Edward and William Henry on the other. The troops which he had appointed for Niagara were the shattered remains of the Forty-fourth and Forty-Eighth, part of his own and of Pepperrell's regiments, four independent regular companies from New York, and a small body of Provincials. The enterprise against Crown Point was assigned to the Provincial forces of New England and New York. Loudoun's instructions seem to have prescribed for him much the same line as Shirley had marked out for himself; but the new commander-in-chief conceived an immense and not wholly unreasonable contempt for Shirley and for all his works.

In the first place, he found that his predecessor had emptied the military chest, and that there was remarkably little to show for the outlay. Oswego, on inspection by a competent engineer, was declared incapable of defence, being ill-designed and incomplete, while the garrison through sickness and neglect was in a shocking condition.[1] The fact was that the king's boats had been used to transport merchandise for sale by private speculators to the Indians, instead of food for the nourishment of the king's troops. Fort William Henry again was found to be in an indescribably filthy state. Graves, slaughterhouses, and latrines were scattered promiscuously about the camp; no discipline was maintained; provisions were scandalously wasted; and the men were dying at the rate of thirty a week. Loudoun decided almost immediately to abandon the attack on Niagara and to turn all his strength against Ticonderoga and Crown Point.

Meanwhile there were sinister rumours that the French were likely to attack Oswego, and Loudoun sent Colonel Webb with the Forty-Fourth regiment to reinforce the garrison. Webb had hardly reached the Great Carrying-place on his way, when the news met him that Oswego had already been captured. On the night of the 9th the Marquis of Montcalm, an energetic officer who had arrived in Canada in May 1755, had swooped down swiftly and secretly upon the fort with three thousand men, and after three days' cannonade had forced it to surrender. Webb at once retired with precipitation, and in alarm at a report that the French were advancing upon New York, burned the fort at the Great Carrying place and retreated down the Mohawk. Such timidity was worthy of Newcastle's nominee; and this disaster brought the whole of the operations to a standstill. Montcalm having burned Oswego retired to Ticonderoga, where with five thousand men he took up a position from which Loudoun could not hope, with the troops at his disposal, to dislodge him.

The British general therefore contented himself with improving the defences of Fort Edward; and therewith ended the campaign of 1756 in North America. Everything had gone as ill as possible. Loudoun had shown great impatience with the Provincials, and the Provincials had taken no pains to help him. In Pennsylvania every conceivable obstacle was thrown in the way of recruiting; in New York there was not less friction over the quartering of the king's troops. There were reasons sufficient in the jealousy, the inexperience, and

1. Loudoun to Fox, 19th and 29th August 1756.

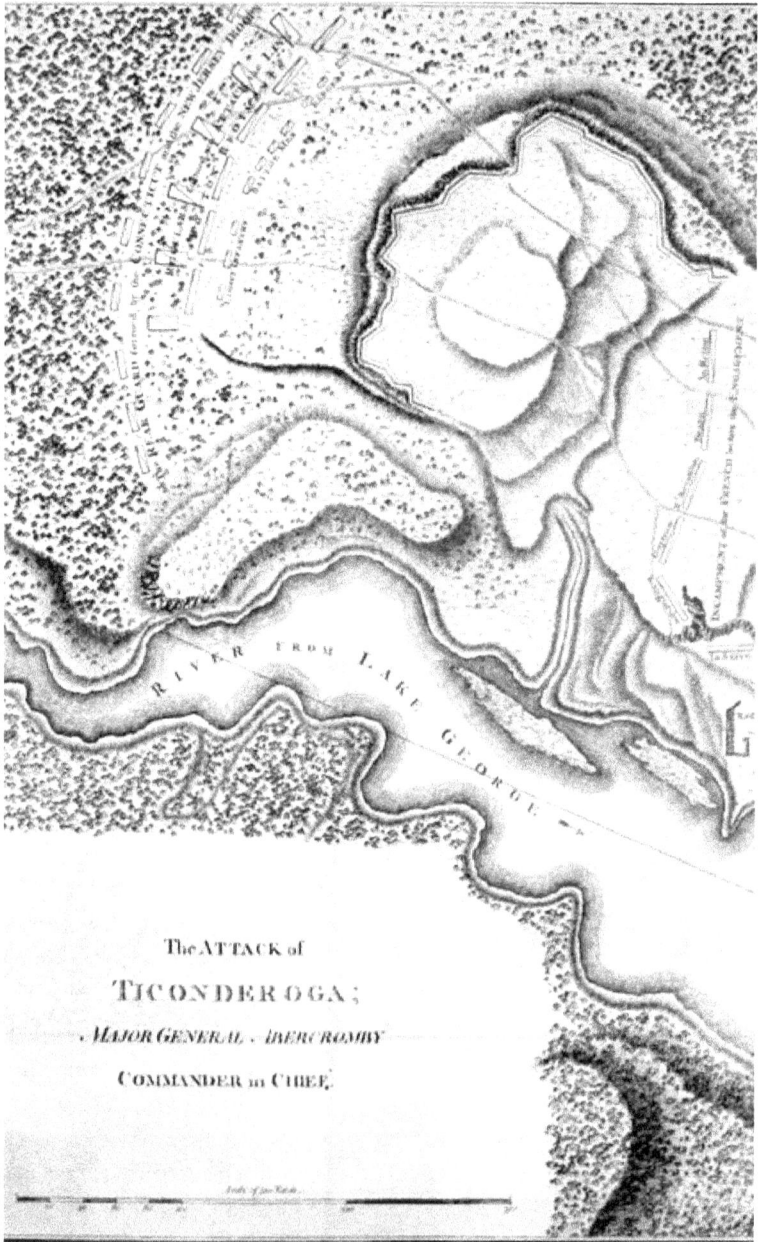

The ATTACK of

TICONDEROGA;

MAJOR GENERAL ABERCROMBY

COMMANDER in CHIEF.

Scale of 500 Yards

ABERCROMBY'S ATTACK ON

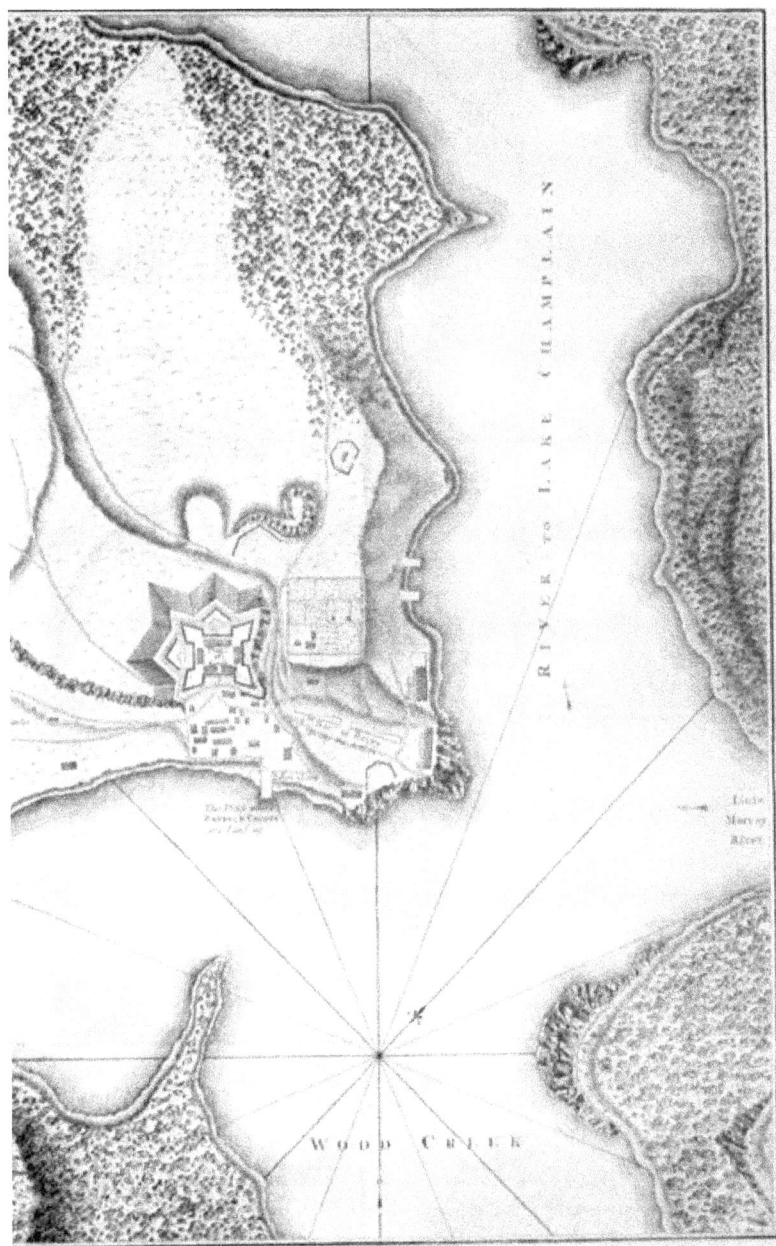

TICONDEROGA, 1758

occasionally the corruption of the Provincials to excuse impatience in the general, but Loudoun was not conciliatory in manner nor had he the ability which commands confidence. He was, in fact, one more of the incompetent men nominated by an incompetent administration. All that he could show for his first campaign was the loss of Oswego, the station which bound the British colonies to the great Indian trade with the West, the place of arms from which the chain of French posts was to be cut in two, in a word the sharpest and deadliest weapon in the armoury of British North America. Small wonder that the French were filled with triumph and the British colonies with dismay.

CHAPTER 8

The Seven Years' War

The news of yet another reverse heaped fuel on the flame of the nation's indignation against Newcastle; but meanwhile the cloud of war which had hung so long in menace over Europe burst at last in one tremendous storm. For some months past a league had been forming between France, Austria, Saxony, Russia, and Sweden to crush Frederick the Great and partition Prussia. France had been launched into this strange alliance by Madame de Pompadour, in revenge for Frederick's disdainful rejection of a friendly message; the *Czarina* likewise sought vengeance for an epigram; Austria burned to recover Silesia; Saxony had been enticed by Austria with the lure of a share in partitioned Prussia; and Sweden had been attracted by the bait of Pomerania.

Frederick, fully aware of all that was going forward, resolved to meet the danger rather than await it, and boldly invading Saxony began the Seven Years' War.[1] Where it should end no man could divine. All that was certain was that Frederick, far from protecting Hanover, would have much ado to defend himself. Thus, then, on the one side there was Hanover open to attack, and on the other Minorca lost, British naval reputation tarnished, and France triumphant in America. Further, though as yet men knew it not, the news of the loss of Calcutta and of the tragedy of the Black Hole was even then on its way across the ocean. The outcry against the government rose to a dangerous height; Fox deserted Newcastle, and resigned; and at length, in November, the shifty old jobber himself, after endless intrigues to retain office, reluctantly and ungracefully made way, nominally for the Duke of Devonshire, but in reality for William Pitt.

On the 2nd of December Parliament met, and the spirit of the

1. *Frederick the Great & the Seven Years' War* by F. W. Longman is also published by Leonaur.

new minister showed itself at once in the speech from the throne. The electoral troops and Hessians were to be sent back forthwith to Germany; and it was now the royal desire, which it had not been before Pitt took office, that the militia should be made more efficient. In a word, England was from henceforth to fight her battles for herself. Two days later leave was granted for the introduction of a Militia Bill, and on the 15th estimates were submitted for a British Establishment of thirty thousand men for the service of Great Britain and nineteen thousand for the colonies, besides two thousand artillery and engineers; the absence of Minorca from its usual place in the list of garrisons providing a significant comment on the whole. Of the additional troops fifteen thousand had already been appointed for enlistment in September, when orders had been issued for the raising of a second battalion to each of fifteen regiments of the Line. [2] These battalions were erected two years later into distinct regiments, of which ten still remain with us, numbered the Sixty-First to the Seventieth.

This addition showed marks of Pitt's influence, but after the Christmas recess his handiwork was seen in a new and daring experiment, namely the formation of two regiments of Highlanders, each eleven hundred strong, which, though afterwards disbanded, became famous under the names of their colonels, Fraser and Montgomery.[3]

The idea was a bold one, for it struck the last weapon from the dying hands of Jacobitism and turned it against itself; and the result soon approved it as a success. The existing Scottish regiments were required to contribute eighty non-commissioned officers who could speak Gaelic; [4] and the Highlander from henceforth took his place not as a subverter of thrones but as a builder of empires. It is remarkable, concurrently, to note the sudden wave of energy which swept over the entire military administration in the first weeks of 1757, when the breath of one great man had once broken the springs and set the stagnant waters aflow.

Shirley's and Pepperrell's regiments, which had been crippled and ruined at Oswego, were struck off the list of the army to make room for more efficient corps. [5] Newcastle's feeble ministers had directed

2. *Miscellaneous Orders*, 20th Sept. 1756. The regiments thus augmented were as follows, the regiments made from their second battalions being added in brackets. 3rd (61st), 4th (62nd), 8th (63rd), 11th (64th), 12th (65th), 19th (66th), 20th (67th), 23rd(68th), 24th (69th), 31st (70th), 32nd, 33rd, 34th, 36th, 37th.

3. Order for raising them, *Miscellaneous Orders*, 4th Jan. 1757.

4. *Secretary's Common Letter Book*, 25th Jan. 1757.

5. *Ibid.*, 22nd Dec. 1756.

the embarkation of a single battalion only, besides drafts, to America: Pitt, without counter-ordering these, ordered the augmentation and despatch of seven battalions more. [6]

The Forty-Ninth regiment, which was serving in Jamaica, was increased to nearly double of its former strength, to hearten the colonists in that island. The Royal Artillery was raised to a total of twenty-four companies and distributed into two battalions, and a company of Miners, first conceived of six months before, was incorporated with it.[7] Finally, the Marines, which had been creeping up in strength ever since the beginning of the war, were augmented from one hundred to one hundred and thirty companies, so that men should not be lacking for the fleet. Nor was it only in the mere activity of departments and ubiquity of recruiting sergeants that the spirit of the master was seen. The nation was stirred by such military ardour as it had not felt since the Civil War, and there was a rush for commissions in the army. [8]

On the re-assembling of Parliament the Militia Bill was again brought forward, and, though it did not pass the Lords until June, was so essential a feature of Pitt's first short administration that it may be dealt with here once and for all. The measure was introduced by George Townsend and was practically identical with that which had been rejected in the previous year, though Henry Conway, an officer of some distinction, had prepared an alternative scheme which was preferred by many. The bill as ultimately passed appointed a proportion of men to be furnished for the Militia in every county of England and Wales, from Devonshire and Middlesex, which were to provide sixteen hundred men apiece, to Anglesey, which was called upon for no more than eighty.

These men were to be chosen by lot from lists drawn up by the parochial authorities for the Lords Lieutenants and their deputies; and every man so chosen was to serve for three years, at the close of which period he was to enjoy exemption until his time should come again. Thus it was designed that every eligible man in succession should pass through the ranks and serve for a fixed term. Special powers were given to justices and to deputy-lieutenants to discharge men from duty on sufficient reason shown, or after two years of service if they were

---

6. *Secretary's Common Letter Book*, 21st Sept. 1756, 29th Jan. 1757. The regiments were the 2nd batt. 1st Foot, 17th, 27th, 28th, 43rd, 46th, 55th Foot.

7. *Warrant Books*, 1st May 1756, 4th March 1757.

8. So I gather from the countless letters on the subject in *Secretary's Common Letter Book*, Jan. and Feb. 1757.

over five-and-thirty years of age. The possession of a certain property was required as a qualification for officers, who likewise were entitled to discharge after four years' service, provided that others could be found to take their places. Provision was also made for the appointment by the king of an adjutant from the regular army to every regiment, and of a sergeant to every twenty men.

The organisation was by regiments of from seven to twelve companies, in which no company was to be of smaller strength than eighty men. The Lord Lieutenant of each county was in command of that county's militia; and in case of urgent danger the king was empowered to embody the whole force, communicating his reasons to Parliament if in session, when officers and men became entitled to the pay of their rank in the army and subject to the articles of war. It had been part of the original design, favoured with reservations by Pitt himself, that Sunday should be a day of exercise, as in Switzerland and other Protestant countries; but this clause was dropped in deference to petitions from several dissenting sects, and it was finally enacted that the men should be drilled in half-companies and whole companies alternately on every Monday from April to October.

The Act was not passed without much opposition in the Lords, who indeed reduced the numbers of the force to thirty-two thousand men, or one-half of the strength voted by the Commons, and added clauses which clogged the working of the measure. Nor was it at first enforced without dangerous riot and tumult in some quarters, due principally to the unscrupulous employment, already narrated, of men enlisted for duty at home on foreign service. Nevertheless the great step was taken. A local force had been established for domestic defence, and the regular army was set free for service abroad, or more truly for the service of conquest.

During the early debates on the Militia Bill Pitt himself was absent, being confined to his house by gout; nor was it until the 17th of February that he appeared in his place to support the royal request for subsidies for Hanover and for the King of Prussia. The occasion drew upon him not a few sarcasms, for no man had more vehemently denounced the turning of Great Britain into a milch cow for the Electorate; but he waived the sneers aside in his wonted imperious fashion, for, consistent or inconsistent, he knew at least his own mind. It was one thing for British interests to be subordinated to Hanoverian; but it was quite another for Britain and Hanover to march shoulder to shoulder against a common enemy for their common advantage. The conquest of America in Germany was, as shall be seen, no idle phrase, though few as yet might comprehend its purport. But suddenly at this point Pitt's career was for the moment checked.

Notwithstanding this proof of his loyalty to the cause of Hanover, the king was still unfriendly towards his new minister, and actually found, in the peril which threatened his beloved Electorate, a pretext for dismissing him from office. In March 1757 a French army of one hundred thousand men poured over the Rhine; and it was necessary to call out the Hanoverian troops to oppose it. The king was urgent for the Duke of Cumberland to command these forces, but the duke was by no means so anxious to accept the trust. The memory of past failure oppressed him; and, since he hated Pitt, he was unwilling to correspond with him or to depend on him for instructions and supplies. To obviate this difficulty the king agreed to remove Pitt; and thus a minister of genius was discarded that an unskilful commander might take the field. It was a proceeding worthier of Versailles than of St. James's.

On the 5th of April Pitt, having refused to resign, received intimation of his dismissal; but by this time the nation had been roused to such a pitch that it would suffer no return to the imbecile and disgraceful administration of the past two years. The stocks fell; all the principal towns in England sent the freedom of their corporations to Pitt, and, in Walpole's phrase, for weeks it rained gold boxes. The king turned to Newcastle, but the contemptible old intriguer tried in vain to form a government with Pitt or without him.

For eleven whole weeks the negotiations continued and the country was left virtually without a government of any kind, until at length it was seen that Pitt's return to office was inevitable, and on the 27th of July, though Newcastle still retained the post of First Lord of the Treasury, Pitt was finally reinstated as Secretary of State on his own terms, that is to say, with full control of the war and of foreign affairs. "I will borrow the duke's majority to carry on the government," he had said, "I am sure that I can save this country and that no one else can."

CHAPTER 9

Disaster at Fort William Henry

This was the turning-point of the whole war; but during the political struggle much precious time had been lost, all enterprise had been paralysed, and all arrangements dislocated. Thus fresh misfortunes were still at hand to increase the new minister's difficulties. In January Loudoun had received the Twenty-second regiment and the draft sent out to him by Newcastle's Government; but in April he was still awaiting his instructions as to the coming campaign, and meanwhile had little to report but the difficulties thrown by the Provincial authorities in the way of recruiting. [1] Pitt's intention, in deference to Loudoun's own representations, had been that he should attack Louisburg; and the seven battalions already referred to had been ordered to sail to Halifax with that object.

These troops had been embarked on the 17th of March but had been detained by contrary winds until after the date of Pitt's dismissal; and though there seems to have been some effort to get them to sea a few days later, it is none the less certain that for one reason or another they did not reach Halifax until July. [2] Meanwhile Loudoun's position was most embarrassing. He had withdrawn all his troops from the frontier to New York, and was waiting only for news of Admiral Holburne's squadron and the reinforcements that he might embark and sail to Halifax to join them. Not a word as to Holburne reached him; and all that he could discover was the unwelcome fact that a French fleet, strong enough to destroy his own escort and sink the whole of his transports, had been seen off the coast. [3] He decided at last that the

---

1. Loudoun to Fox, 25th Jan.; to Pitt, 25th April 1757.
2. Pitt's instructions to General Hopson, 19th Feb.; Holderness to Loudoun, 8th April, 2nd May; Loudoun to Holderness, 5th August 1757.
3. Loudoun to Pitt, 30th May 1757.

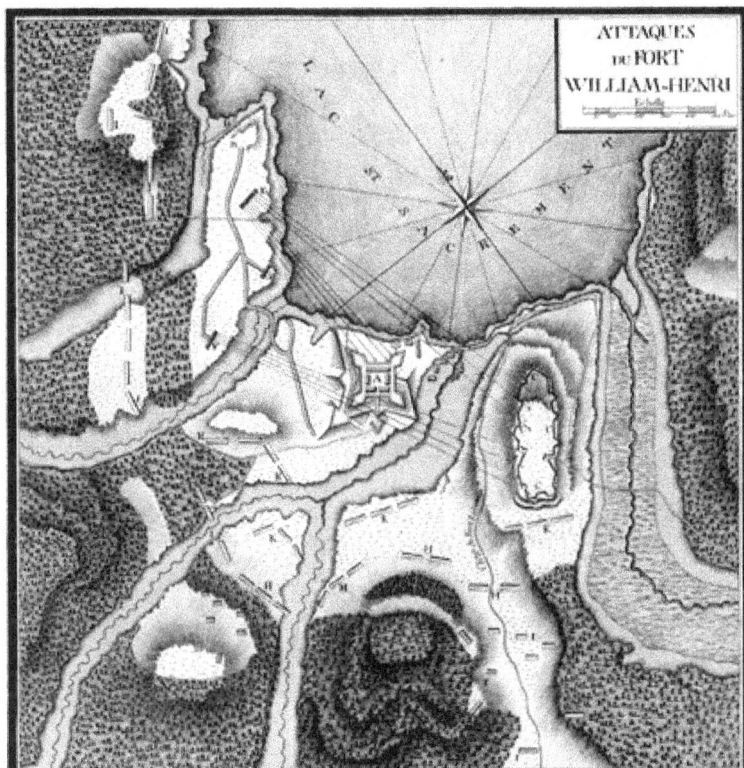

ATTAQUES
DU FORT
WILLIAM-HENRI

ATTAQUES DU FORT WILLIAM-HENRI
en Amérique
par les troupes françaises, aux ordres du Marquis de Montcalm.
Prise de ce fort le 7 Août 1757.

RENVOI

A. Fort William-Henri B. Ouverture des tranchées la nuit du 4 au 5 Août
C. Camp retranché que les anglais allèrent occuper lors de l'arrivée des français
D. Baie où les français débarquèrent leur artillerie. E. Batterie de huit
canons & d'un mortier F. Batterie de dix canons & d'un mortier G. Batterie
de six pièces, dont on ne fit aucun usage H. Position de Mr. de Lévis
pendant l'investissement du fort I. Position des troupes durant le siège
K. Leur position après la prise pendant la démolition des retranchemens
faits par les anglais ▬▬▬ Troupes sauvages

C P & C M

risk must be run, embarked his troops and arrived safely at Halifax, where ten days later he was joined by Holburne's squadron.

The troops were landed, and then, but not till then, steps were taken to obtain intelligence as to the condition of Louisburg. This fact alone enables us to judge of Loudoun's efficiency as a commander. The first reports received, though meagre, were encouraging, and the troops were re-embarked for action; but directly afterwards an intercepted letter revealed the fact that twenty-two French sail of the line were in Louisburg harbour, and that the garrison had been increased to seven thousand men. The French naval force was so far superior to Holburne's that any attempt to prosecute the enterprise was hopeless. The expedition was therefore abandoned, and the troops sailed back to New York.

Meanwhile the disarming of the frontier afforded Montcalm[4] an opportunity for striking a telling blow. At the end of July eight thousand French, Canadians and Indians were assembled at Ticonderoga, and on the 30th twenty-five hundred of them under command of an officer named Lévis started to march to North-West Bay on the western shore of Lake George, while Montcalm with five thousand more embarked in *bateaux* on Lake Champlain. On the following day both divisions united close to Fort William Henry, and on the 3rd of August Montcalm, mindful of the defeat of Dieskau, laid siege to the fort in form. Fort William Henry was an irregular bastioned square, built of crossed logs filled up with earth and mounting seventeen guns.

On the northern side it was protected by the lake, on the eastern side by a marsh, and to south and west by ditches and *chevaux de frise*. The garrison, which had been reinforced a few days before in view of coming trouble, counted a total strength of twenty-two hundred men, including regular troops, sailors and mechanics, under the command of a veteran Scottish officer, Lieutenant-Colonel Monro of the Thirty-Fifth Foot. On the night of the 4th the trenches were opened on the western side of the fort, and two days later the French batteries opened fire. The fort returned the fire with spirit, but it was evident that unless it were speedily relieved its fall could be only a question of time. Colonel Webb lay only fourteen miles away at Fort Edward, and by summoning troops hurriedly from New York and from the posts on the Mohawk had collected a force of over four thousand men; but Montcalm was reported to have twelve thousand men, and Webb did

4. *Montcalm at the Battle of Carillon (Ticonderoga) (July 8th, 1758)* by Maurice Sautai is also published by Leonaur.

not think it prudent to advance to Lake George until further rein-forced. He therefore sent a letter to Monro, advising him to make the best terms that he could, which was intercepted by Montcalm and po-litely forwarded by him to its destination. The siege was pushed vigor-ously forward, and by the 8th the besieged were in desperate straits.

Over three hundred men had been killed and wounded, all the guns excepting a few small pieces had been disabled, and, worst of all, smallpox was raging in the fort. On the 9th, therefore, Monro ca-pitulated on honourable terms, which provided, among other condi-tions, that the French should escort the garrison to Fort Edward. On the march the Indian allies of the French burst in upon the unarmed British, unchecked by the Canadian militia, and despite the efforts of Montcalm and of his officers massacred eighty of them and maltreated many more. This, however, though it might well stir the vengeful feel-ings of the British, was but an episode. The serious facts were the loss of the post at Lake George, and yet another British reverse in North America.

Such were among the last legacies bequeathed by Newcastle's fee-bleness; and meanwhile the king's perversity in driving Pitt from office had brought speedy judgment upon himself and upon Cumberland. The duke was defeated by the French at the Battle of Hastenbeck, and retreating upon Stade concluded, or rather found concluded for him, the convention of Klosterzeven, whereby he agreed to evacuate the country. Such were the discouragements which confronted Pitt on resuming office.

It was hard to see how he could initiate any operations of value at so late a period of the year, but there was one species of diversion which, though little recommended by experience of the past, lay open to him still, namely a descent upon the French coast. A young Scot-tish officer, who had travelled in France, gave intelligence based on no very careful or recent observation, that the fortifications of Rochefort were easily assailable; and Pitt on the receipt of this intelligence at once conceived the design of surprising Rochefort and burning the ships in the Charente below it. Somewhat hastily it was determined to send ten of the best battalions and a powerful fleet on this enterprise, and the military command was offered to Lord George Sackville, who not relishing the task found an excuse for declining. Pitt was then for entrusting it to General Henry Conway, but the king objected to this officer on the score of his youth, and insisted on setting over him Sir John Mordaunt, a veteran who had showed merit in the past, but had

MONTCALM ATTEMPTS TO PREVENT OUTRAGES AT FORT WILLIAM HENRY

now lost his nerve and was conscious that he had lost it. He and Conway alike objected to the project as based on flimsy and insufficient information, but both thought themselves bound in honour to accept the trust confided to them.

Though the expedition had been decided upon in July, it was not until two months later that it sailed from England, and meanwhile the troops waited as usual in the Isle of Wight. [5] There was much delay in providing transports, and the embarkation was so ill-managed that the troops were obliged to row a full mile to their ships. On the 8th of September, however, the vessels put to sea under convoy of sixteen sail of the line under Sir Edward Hawke, and after much delay from foul winds and calms anchored in Basque Roads, the haven which was to become famous half a century later for an attack of a very different kind.

On the 23rd the fortifications of the Isle d'Aix were battered down by the fleet and the island itself captured; but therewith the operations came abruptly to an end. Fresh information revealed that the French were fully prepared to meet an attack on Rochefort; and a council of war decided that any attempt to take it by escalade would be hopeless. It was therefore decided to attack the forts at the mouth of the Charente, but the order was countermanded by Mordaunt; and after a week's delay Hawke gave the General to understand that unless operations were prosecuted forthwith he would return with the fleet to England

The military commanders thereupon decided that they would return with him, which on the 1st of October they did, to the huge indignation of both fleet and army. A court of inquiry was held over this absurd issue to such extensive and costly preparations, and Sir John Mordaunt was tried by court-martial but honourably acquitted. The incident gave rise to a fierce war of pamphlets. It is certain that Mordaunt showed remarkable supineness, and he was suspected of a wish to injure the influence of Pitt by turning the enterprise into ridicule; but with such men as Wolfe, Conway and Cornwallis among the senior officers, the only conclusion is that, in the view of military men, no object of the least value could have been gained by any operations whatever. Military opinion had been against the expedition from the first. Ligonier, a daring officer but of ripe experience and sound judgment, wrote of it in the most lukewarm terms as likely to lead to nothing.

5. The regiments were the 3rd, 5th, 8th, 15th, 20th, 24th, 25th, 30th, 50th, 51st.

81

MONTCALM ATTEMPTS TO PREVENT OUTRAGES AT FORT WILLIAM HENRY

On the whole it seems that the troops were sent on a fool's errand, and that the blame lay solely with Pitt. The nation was furious, and the king showed marked coldness towards the generals who had taken part in the failure; but Pitt, who was more hurt and disappointed than any one, took no step except to promote Wolfe,[6] who had advocated active measures, over the heads of several other officers, and thus in one way at least extracted good from evil.

So ended the campaigning season of 1757 with an unbroken record of ill success in every quarter. But the right man was now at the head of affairs and was looking about him for the right instruments. The long period of darkness had come to an end and the light was about to break, at first in flickering broken rays, but soon to shine out in one blaze of dazzling and surpassing splendour.

---

6. *Commanders of the French & Indian War, The Winning of Canada, a Chronicle of Wolfe* and *The Passing of New France, a Chronicle of Montcalm* by William Wood is also published by Leonaur.

MAJOR-GENERAL JAMES WOLFE

CHAPTER 10

Louisburg

Pitt had now a free hand for the execution of such enterprises as he might desire, a freer hand indeed than any of his predecessors for ten years past had enjoyed; for Cumberland, being ill-received by the king on his return from Hastenbeck, had resigned the commandership-in-chief and all his military appointments of whatever description. Pitt, conscious that the duke had been hardly treated, made no secret of his sympathy with him; but there can be no doubt that Ligonier, who succeeded him as commander in chief, was infinitely more competent as a military adviser and more sympathetic as a military colleague. And there was need for sound military capacity to deal with all the projects that were ripening in the minister's teeming brain.

Parliament met on the 1st of December, and the king's speech, after announcing vigorous prosecution of the war in America and elsewhere, begged for support for the King of Prussia. Frederick fortunately stood just at that moment at his highest in the public view, for his two masterly victories at Rossbach and Leuthen; and Parliament did not hesitate to confirm a subsidy to him to enable him to carry on the struggle. But in other respects Pitt could find little to boast of in the past year, and he was obliged to confine his eulogy to Frederick and to Clive, whose victory at Plassey, now just become known in England, could not be ascribed to any extraordinary efforts on the part of a British Ministry. The word "elsewhere" in the king's speech was understood to signify Hanover, though Pitt warmly disclaimed any such interpretation of the term; but the Commons did not quarrel with it nor with the estimates that were submitted in support of the policy.

These were presented on the 7th of December and showed a force for the British Establishment of eighty-six thousand five hundred men, thirty thousand of them for Gibraltar and the colonies, and the remainder nominally for service at home. Four thousand of this number, however, were invalids, who were kept for duties in garrison only, a system wisely copied from earlier days and followed from the beginning to the end of the war. One new regiment only had been raised since the formation of Fraser's and Montgomery's Highlanders,[1] namely Colonel Draper's, which had been created for service in India and which brought up the number of the regiments of the Line to seventy-nine. Adding the troops on the Irish to those on the British Establishment the full numbers of the Army may be set down roughly at one hundred thousand men. It was soon to be seen what Pitt could accomplish with them, when he had found officers who would fulfil his instructions.

America first occupied his attention and was dealt with summarily. The first thing to be done was to recall Lord Loudoun from the command, a resolution which was carried out before the year's end,[2] and to appoint a new general in his place. The choice fell upon General James Abercromby, who had been sent out by Newcastle's Administration; and the selection was not a fortunate one. The next step was to summon Colonel Jeffery Amherst from Germany, where he had been employed since 1756 as Commissary to the Hessian troops in the pay of England. Amherst, it will be remembered, was a Guardsman, and was last seen by us as Ligonier's *aide-de-camp* on the field of Fontenoy; so it is at least probable that his appointment was due to Ligonier's influence.

Three new brigadiers were nominated to serve under him, Lawrence, Whitmore, and James Wolfe. The operations to be undertaken in America were threefold. First and foremost Louisburg was to be besieged; and this duty was assigned to Amherst with fourteen thousand regular troops. Concurrently an advance was to be made upon Crown Point, and pushed forward if possible to Montreal and Quebec; which service was entrusted to Abercromby, aided by Brigadier Lord Howe, with about ten thousand regulars and twenty thousand Provincial troops. Lastly, nineteen hundred regular troops and five thousand Provincials under Brigadier-General Forbes were to repair Braddock's failure and capture Fort Duquêsne.[3]

---

1. *The Black Watch at Ticonderoga* by Frederick B. Richards is also published by Leonaur.
2. Pitt to Loudoun, 20th Dec. 1757.
3. Abercromby's instructions, 30th Dec. 1757.

The number of Provincial troops to be employed was five times as great as that provided by the colonies in any previous year; but Pitt, while asking for so formidable a force, agreed to supply the troops with tents, provisions, arms, and ammunition, leaving to the provinces the expenses of raising, clothing, and paying them only. Moreover, he had readjusted the former regulations as to the seniority of Provincial and Imperial officers, which had given much offence, in a spirit somewhat less to the prejudice of the Provincials. True to his principle that British battles should be fought by British subjects he grudged no expense to gather recruits from the new British beyond sea.

The troops were to be escorted to America by a fleet under Admiral Boscawen, which was strong enough to overpower any French fleet in American waters. A squadron was also sent under Admiral Osborne to the Mediterranean to intercept any French reinforcements from Toulon, while yet another squadron under Sir Edward Hawke cruised with the like object before Rochefort. Osborne's name has been forgotten, and Hawke's lesser services have been swallowed up in the fame of his action before Quiberon; but it may be said here once for all that both officers performed their parts with admirable ability and signal success. The reader may now begin to judge of Pitt's talent for organising victory.

Boscawen, with twenty-three ships of the line and several smaller vessels, sailed with his convoy of transports on the 19th of February. It had been Pitt's hope that the siege of Louisburg should have been begun by the 20th of April; [4] but fate was against him, and the Admiral did not reach Halifax until the 9th of May. Amherst, who had sailed with Captain George Rodney in H.M.S. *Dublin* on the 16th of March, was not less unlucky in his passage; and Boscawen, after waiting for his arrival at Halifax until the 28th of May, at last put to sea without him, but fortunately met the *Dublin* just outside the harbour. The huge fleet, one hundred and fifty-seven sail in all, with eleven thousand troops on board, then steered eastward, and on the 2nd of June sailed into Gabarus Bay, immediately to westward of the tongue of land whereon stood Louisburg.

Here there were three possible landing-places: Freshwater Cove, four miles from the town; Flat Point, which was rather nearer; and White Point, which was within a mile of the ramparts. East of the fortress there was yet another landing-place named Lorambec. It was determined to threaten all these points simultaneously, Lawrence and

4. Abercromby's instructions.

Whitmore with their respective brigades moving towards White Point and Flat Point, with one regiment detached against Lorambec, while Wolfe's brigade should make a true attack upon Freshwater Cove.[5] Nothing very clear was known of the French defences erected to cover these landing-places, and it so happened that the point selected for attack was the most strongly defended of all.

For five days all attempts at disembarkation were frustrated by fog and storm; but at two o'clock on the morning of the 8th the troops were got into the boats, and at daybreak the frigates of the fleet stood in and opened a fierce fire upon the French entrenchments at all of the threatened points. A quarter of an hour later the boats shoved off and pulled for the shore. Wolfe's party consisted of five companies of grenadiers, a body of five hundred and fifty marksmen drawn from the different regiments and known as the Light Infantry, and a body of American Rangers, with Fraser's Highlanders and eight more companies of grenadiers in support. The beach at Freshwater Cove, for which they were making, was a quarter of a mile long, with rocks at each end; and on the shore above it more than a thousand Frenchmen lay behind entrenchments, which were further covered by abatis. Eight cannon and swivels had been brought into position to sweep every portion of the beach and of its approaches, but were cunningly masked by young evergreen shrubs planted in the ground before them. The French had not been at fault when they selected the point remotest from the town as the most likely to be attacked by an enemy.

The boats were close in-shore before the French made any sign, when they suddenly opened a deadly fire of grape and musketry. Wolfe, seeing that a landing in face of such a tempest of shot would be hopeless, signalled to the boats to sheer off; but three of them, filled with Light Infantry on the extreme right, being little exposed to the fire, pulled on to a craggy point just to eastward of the beach, which was sheltered from the enemy's cannon by a small projecting spit. There the three officers in charge leaped ashore followed by their men, and Wolfe hastened the rest of his boats to the same spot. Major Scott, who commanded the Light Infantry, was the first to reach the land; and though his boat was stove in against the rocks he scrambled

---

5. The order of Amherst's force in brigades was as follows, the regiments being enumerated from right to left. Right Brigade (Whitmore), 1 batt. 1st Foot, 40th, 3rd batt. 60th, 48th, 22nd. Centre Brigade (Wolfe), 17th, 47th, 2nd batt. 60th, 35th. Left Brigade (Lawrence), 28th, 58th, Fraser's Highlanders, 45th, 15th.—*Enclosure* in Amherst's letter to Pitt, 11th June 1758.

ashore, and with no more than ten men held his own against six times his numbers of French and Indians, till other troops came to his support.

The rest of the boats followed close in his wake. Many were stove in and not a few capsized; some of the men too were caught by the surf and drowned; but the greater part made their way ashore wet or dry, Wolfe, who was armed only with a cane, leaping into the surf and scrambling over the crags with the foremost. Arrived at the firm ground beyond, the men formed, attacked the nearest French battery in flank, and quickly carried it with the bayonet. Lawrence's brigade now rowed up, and finding the French fully occupied with Wolfe, landed at the western end of the beach with little difficulty or loss. Amherst followed him; and the French seeing themselves attacked on right and left, and fearing to be cut off from the town, abandoned all their guns, some three-and-thirty pieces great and small, and fled into the woods in the rear of their entrenchments.

The British pursued, until on emerging from the forest they found themselves in a cleared space with the guns of Louisburg opening fire upon them. Then the pursuit was checked, for the first great object had been obtained. The total loss of the British little exceeded one hundred in killed, wounded, and drowned; that of the French was not much greater, but the British had gained a solid success. Amherst pitched his camp just beyond range of the guns of the fortress, and selected Flat Point Cove as the place for landing his guns and stores. The disembarkation of material was a task of extreme difficulty and danger owing to the surf, so much so that over one hundred boats were stove in during the course of the siege. The general, therefore, had ample leisure to examine the ground before him. The harbour of Louisburg is a land-locked bay with an extreme width from north-east to south-west of about two and a half miles. The entrance is rather more than a mile wide, but is narrowed to less than half of that distance by a chain of rocky islets. The defences of the entrance were a battery on a small island on the west side of the channel and a fort on the eastern shore at the promontory of Lighthouse Point.

Within the harbour on the northern shore had stood a battery known as the Grand battery, but this was destroyed by the French on the night of Amherst's landing; and on the western shore on a triangular peninsula stood Louisburg itself, the Dunkirk of America, the apex of the triangle pointing towards the harbour, the base towards the land where Amherst's force now lay encamped. The full circuit of its fortifications was about a mile and a half, and the number of cannon and mortars mounted thereon and on the outworks exceeded two hundred. The garrison consisted of five battalions of regular troops, numbering about four thousand men, together with several companies of colonial troops from Canada; the whole being under command of a gallant officer named Drucour.

Finally, at anchor in the harbour lay five ships of the line and seven frigates. The strongest front of the fortress was on the side of the land, running from the sea on the south to the harbour on the north: it was made up of four bastions called in succession, from north to south, the Dauphin's, King's, Queen's, and Princess's bastions. The King's bastion formed part of the citadel, and before it the glacis sloped down to a marsh which protected it completely; but at both extremities of the line there was high ground favourable for the works of a besieging force. It was towards the northern extremity, from a hillock at the edge of the marsh, that Amherst resolved to push his first attack.

Meanwhile the labour to be accomplished before the guns and stores could be brought to the spot was immense. The distance from the landing-place was a mile and a half, every yard of it consisting of deep mud covered with moss and water-weeds, through which it was necessary to make not only a road but an *epaulement* also, to protect the road; for a French frigate, the *Aréthuse*, lay in a lagoon called the Barachois at the extreme western corner of the harbour, and swept all the ground before the ramparts with a flanking fire. While, therefore, this work was going forward Wolfe was ordered with twelve hundred men and artillery to the battery at Lighthouse Point, which had been abandoned by the French, in order to fire upon the Island battery and upon the ships in the harbour. After some days the Island battery was silenced with the help of the fleet, and the men of war were driven under the guns of the main fortress. The entrance to the harbour being thus laid open to the British fleet, the French commander under cover of a foggy night sank six large ships in the channel to bar the passage anew.

On the very day when Wolfe succeeded in silencing the Island battery Amherst's preparations were at last completed; and the British began to break ground on the appointed hillock. From thence the trenches were carried, despite the fire of the *Aréthuse*, towards the Barachois; and it was soon evident that the frigate would be repaid for all the mischief that she had wrought. At the same time Wolfe broke ground to the south opposite to the Princess's bastion, and despite a fierce sortie made by a drunken party of the garrison, pushed his works steadily forward against it. Another three weeks saw the net closing tighter and the fire raining fiercer about the doomed fortress.

The *Aréthuse*, after sticking to her moorings right gallantly under an ever increasing fire, was compelled at last to shift her position. Two days later Wolfe, as busy at the left as at the right attack, made a dash at nightfall upon some rising ground only three hundred yards before the Dauphin's bastion, drove out the French that occupied it, and would not be forced back by the fiercest fire from the ramparts. On the 21st a lucky shell fell on one of the French line-of-battle ships and set her on fire. The scanty crew left on board of her could not check the flames. She drifted from her moorings upon two of her consorts and kindled them also; and all three were burned to the water's edge. The two remaining line-of-battle ships survived them but a little time, for a few nights later six hundred sailors rowed silently into the harbour and surprised and captured both of them, One, being aground, was burned, and the other was towed off, in contempt of the fire from the fortress, to a safe anchorage.

By this time Amherst's batteries had reduced Louisburg almost to defencelessness. The masonry of the fortress had crumbled under the concussion of its own guns and was little able to stand the shot of the British. A new battery erected on the hill to the north of the Barachois raked the western front of the French works from end to end, and there was no standing against its fire. On the 26th of July the last gun on that front was silenced and a practicable breach had been made. Drucour then made overtures for a capitulation. Amherst's reply was short and stern: the garrison must surrender as prisoners of war, and a definite answer must be returned within one hour.

Drucour replied at first with defiance, but, before his messenger could reach Amherst he sent a second emissary to accept the terms; and on the following day the British occupied the fortress. The casualties of the besiegers were not heavy, little exceeding five hundred killed and wounded of all ranks. The loss of the French is unknown, but must have been very great, from sickness not less than from shot and shell. The number of soldiers and sailors made prisoners amounted to fifty-six hundred, while over two hundred cannon and a large quantity of munitions and stores were surrendered with the fortress. So Cape Breton, and Prince Edward's Island with it, passed under the dominion of the British for ever.

The siege over, Amherst proposed to Boscawen to proceed to

Quebec, but the admiral did not consider the enterprise to be feasible. Drucour's gallant defence, indeed, had accomplished one object, in preventing Amherst from co-operating with Abercromby in the attack on Canada; though, could the siege have been begun at the date fixed by Pitt, his efforts would have been of little avail. Amherst therefore left four battalions to garrison Louisburg, [6] and sent Colonel Monckton, Colonel Lord Rollo, and Wolfe, each with a sufficient force, to complete the work of subjugation on Prince Edward's Island, the Bay of Fundy, and the Gulf of St. Lawrence. Wolfe having accomplished his part of the task went home on sick leave, and Amherst sailed with five battalions [7] for Boston, where he arrived on the 14th of September and was received with immense though rather inconvenient enthusiasm by the inhabitants. [8] His presence was but too sorely needed to repair the mischief wrought by Abercromby's incapacity.

---

6. The 22nd, 28th, 40th and 45th.
7. The 1st, 17th, 47th, 48th, Fraser's Highlanders.
8. "I could not prevent the men from being filled with rum by the inhabitants." Amherst to Pitt, 18th September 1758.

CHAPTER 11

The Debacle of Ticonderoga

The prospects of Abercromby at the opening of the campaign were such as might have encouraged any general. Vaudreuil, the Governor of Canada, a corrupt and incapable man, knowing of the intended advance of the British by Lakes George and Champlain upon Ticonderoga and Crown Point, had proposed to avert it by a counter-raid along the Mohawk upon the Hudson. This plan, being vague, and indeed impracticable, was abandoned; and the defence of the approaches to Montreal was committed to Montcalm, who was stationed at Ticonderoga with an insufficient force of about four thousand men, and without support from the posts higher up the lake. To Abercromby, with seven thousand regular troops and nine thousand Provincials, the exposure of this weak and isolated force should have been welcome as the solution of all his difficulties. It must now be seen to what end he turned so excellent an opportunity.

The early months of the summer were occupied with the task, always vexatious and troublesome, of collecting the Provincial troops, and of sending supplies up the Mohawk and the Hudson to Fort Edward. The latter work was tedious and harassing, despite the facilities of carriage by water, for there were three portages between Albany and Fort Edward, at each of which all boats had to be unladen, and dragged, together with their stores, for three or even more miles overland before they could be launched again for easier progress. None the less the business went forward with great energy; and notwithstanding the danger of convoys from the attack of Indians when passing through the forest, the work of escorting was so perfectly managed that not one was molested. These admirable arrangements were due to Brigadier Lord Howe, the eldest of three brothers, all of whom were destined to leave a mark for good or evil on English history.

Howe had been appointed by Pitt to make good the failings which were suspected in Abercromby. He was now thirty-four years of age, and having arrived in America with his regiment, the Fifty-fifth, in the previous year, had been at pains to learn the art of forest-warfare from the most famous leader of the Provincial irregulars. He threw off all training and prejudices of the barrack-yard, joined the irregulars in their scouting-parties, shared the hardships and adopted the dress of his rough companions and became one of themselves. Having thus schooled himself he began to impart the lessons that he had learned to his men. He made officers and men, alike of regular and of Provincial troops, throw off all useless encumbrances; he cut the skirts off their coats and the hair off their heads, browned the barrels of their muskets, clad their lower limbs in leggings to protect them from briars, and filled the empty space in their knapsacks with thirty pounds of meal, so as to make them independent for weeks together of convoys of supplies.

In a word, he headed a reaction against the stiff unpractical school of Germany so much favoured by Cumberland, and tried to equip men reasonably for the rough work that lay before them. Such ideas had occurred to other men besides him. Colonel Bouquet[1] of the Sixtieth wished to dress his men like Indians, and Brigadier Forbes went cordially with him, for, as he wrote emphatically, "We must learn the art of war from the Indians."

Washington, again, said that if the matter were left to his inclination he would put both men and officers into Indian dress and set the example himself. [2] There was in fact a general revolt of all practical men against powder and pipe-clay for bush-fighting, and Howe was fortunately in a position to turn it to account. Possibly it is to his influence that may be traced the formation in the same year of a regiment which, being designed for purposes of scouting and skirmishing only, was clothed in dark brown skirtless goats without lace of any description. This corps ranked for a time as the eightieth of the Line, and was known as Gage's Light Infantry. [3]

It must not be supposed that these reforms were accepted without demur. Officers were dismayed to find that they were expected to

1. *Bouquet & the Ohio Indian War,* two accounts of Indian warfare in 18th century America by Cyrus Cort & William Smith is also published by Leonaur.
2. Forbes to Bouquet, 27th June; Washington to Bouquet, 3rd July 1758. *Bouquet Papers,* Add. M.S. 21640, 21641.
3. *Board of General Officers, Letter Book,* vol. ccclx.

wash their own clothes without the help of the regimental women, and to carry their own knives and forks with them according to Howe's example; and the German soldiers, of whom there were many in the Sixtieth, sorely resented the cropping of their heads. But Howe was a strict disciplinarian, and not the less, but rather the more, on this account was adored by the men. [4]

By the end of June the whole of Abercromby's force, with all its supplies, was assembled at the head of Lake George. On the 4th of July the stores were shipped, and on the following day the men were embarked. The arrangements were perfect: each corps marched to its appointed place on the beach without the least confusion, and before the sun was well arisen the whole army was afloat. The scene was indescribably beautiful. Overhead the sky was blue and cloudless; the sun had just climbed above the mountain tops, and his rays slanted down over the vast rolling slope of forest to the lake. Not a breath of air was moving to ruffle the still blue water or stir the banks of green; leaves around it, as the twelve hundred boats swept over the glassy surface.

Robert Rogers,[5] most famous of American partisans and instructor of Howe, with his rangers, and Gage with part of his new Light Infantry led the way. John Bradstreet of New England followed next with the boatmen, himself the best boatman among them; and then in three long parallel columns came the main body of the army. To right and left blue coats showed the presence of the Provincial troops of New England and New York, and in the centre flared the well-known English scarlet. Howe led this centre column with the Fifty-Fifth, his own regiment; and after him followed the first and fourth battalions of the Sixtieth, the Twenty-Seventh, Forty-Fourth, Forty-Sixth, and last of all the Forty-Second with their sombre tartan, each regiment marked by its flying colours of green or buff or yellow or crimson.

Then, unmarked by any flag, for colours they had none, came more of Gage's brown coats. Two "floating castles" armed with artillery also accompanied this column, towering high above the slender canoes and whale-boats; and in the rear came the *bateaux* laden with

4. Horatio Gates to Bouquet, 8th September 1759. "Lord Howe was mistaken in cropping the Germans. Some, nay, many of them, would sooner have parted with their scalps than with their plaited tails to be trimmed *a la sauvage*" *Bouquet Papers*.
5. *Journals of Robert Rogers of the Rangers*, the exploits of Rogers & the Rangers in his own words during 1755-1761 in the French & Indian War by Robert Rogers is also published by Leonaur.

Major Robert Rogers

stores and baggage, with a rear-guard made up of red coats and of blue. So the great armament, stretching almost from shore to shore, crept on over the bosom of the lake, the strains of fife and drum mingling with the plashing of ten thousand oars, till the narrows were reached and the broad front dwindled into a slender procession six miles in length, still creeping on like some huge sinuous serpent on its errand of destruction and death.

By five in the afternoon the flotilla had travelled five-and-twenty miles, and a halt was made for the baggage and artillery, which had lagged behind. At eleven o'clock it started again, and at daybreak reached the narrow channel that leads into Lake Champlain by the headland of Ticonderoga. A small advanced post of the French on the shore was driven back, and the work of disembarkation was begun. By noon the whole army had been landed on the western shore of the lake; Rogers with his rangers was sent forward to reconnoitre, and the troops were formed in four columns for the march. The route proposed was to follow the western bank of the channel which connects Lake George with Lake Champlain, since the French had destroyed the bridge over it, and to fall upon Ticonderoga from the rear. The way lay through virgin forest, encumbered with thick undergrowth and strewed with the decaying trunks and limbs of fallen trees. All order became impossible; the men struggled forward as best they could; the columns got mixed together; the guides lost all idea of their direction in the maze; and the army for a time was lost in the forest.

Meanwhile the French advanced party, some three hundred and fifty men, which had fallen back before the British, found its retreat cut off, and had no resource but to take to the woods. They too lost themselves among the trees, and the two hostile bodies were groping their way helplessly on, when the right centre column of the British, with Lord Howe and some rangers at its head, blundered unawares full upon the French party. A sharp skirmish followed, and in the general confusion the main body of the British, hearing volleys but unable to see, became very unsteady. Fortunately the rangers stood firm, and Rogers' advanced guard, turning back at the sound of shots, caught the French between two fires and virtually annihilated them. The British loss in this affair was trifling in numbers but none the less fatal to the expedition; for Lord Howe lay dead with a bullet through his heart, and with his death the whole soul of the army expired.

Abercromby's force was for the moment paralysed. Half of his army was lost, nor did he know where to find it. So much of it as he could collect he kept under arms all night, and next morning he fell back to his landing-place, where to his great relief he found the rest of his troops awaiting him. Montcalm meanwhile had been devoured by anxiety. The channel between Lake George and Lake Champlain being impassable by boats owing to rapids, the usual route to Ticonderoga lay across it by some saw-mills at the foot of the rapids, where he had already destroyed the bridge. Nevertheless it was not by these saw-mills but on the western bank of the channel that he had determined to make his stand; nor was it until the evening of the 6th that, yielding to the advice of two of his officers, he decided to retire to Ticonderoga. Accordingly, at noon of the 7th, Abercromby sent Rogers forward with a detachment to occupy the saw-mills. The bridge was rebuilt; and the army, crossing the channel late in the afternoon, occupied the camp deserted by the French. Abercromby was now within two miles of Ticonderoga.

But meanwhile Montcalm had not been idle. The peninsula of Ticonderoga consists of a rocky plateau with low ground on each side, standing at the junction of Lakes George and Champlain. The fort stood near the end of this peninsula; and half a mile to westward of the spot the ground rises and forms a ridge across the plateau. On this ridge Montcalm decided at the last moment to throw up abatis and accept battle. The outline of the works had already been traced, and at the dawn of the 7th every man of his force was at work, cutting down the trees that covered the ground. The tops were cut off and the logs piled into a massive breast-work nine feet high, which was carefully loop-holed. The forest before the breastwork was also felled and left lying with the tops turned outwards, as though, to use the words of an eye-witness, it had been laid low by a hurricane. Between these felled trees and the breast-work the ground was covered with heavy boughs, their points being sharpened and the branches interlaced, so as to present an almost impenetrable obstacle. The French officers themselves were amazed at the work which had been accomplished in one day.

Still the position was no Malplaquet, and there was no occasion for Abercromby to dread it. It was open to him either to attack Montcalm in his flanks, which were unfortified; or to bring up his artillery and batter the breast-work to splinters about his ears; or better still to post his guns on a height, called Mount Defiance, which commanded the position, and to rake the breastwork from end to end; or best of all to mask this improvised stronghold with a part of his force and push on with the rest northward up Lake Champlain and so cut off at once Montcalm's supplies and his retreat. The French general had but thirty-six hundred men and only eight days' provisions with him, so that this movement would have ensured his surrender without the firing of a shot. Abercromby's intelligence, however, told him that the French were six thousand strong and that three thousand more were expected to join them at any hour; and he was nervously anxious to make his attack before this reinforcement, which had in reality no existence, should arrive on the spot.

Accordingly, at dawn of the 8th, Abercromby sent his engineers to reconnoitre the enemy's position from Mount Defiance. The duty was most perfunctorily fulfilled, and the chief engineer, Lieutenant-Colonel Clark, reported that the works could be captured by direct assault. This was enough for Abercromby. Without further inquiry he resolved that the artillery should be left idle at the place where it had been landed, and that the abatis should be carried with the bayonet.

It was high noon, and the French were still busily strengthening their wooden ramparts with earth and sandbags when shots in the forest before them gave warning that the British advanced parties had struck against their picquets. Instantly they fell in behind the breast-work, three deep, eight battalions of regular troops and four hundred and fifty Canadians, numbering in all little more than a fourth of the British force. The advance of the British was covered by the Light Infantry and rangers while the columns of attack were forming under shelter of the forest. Then the skirmishers cleared the front and the scarlet masses came forward, solid and steady; the picquets leading, the grenadiers in support, the battalions of the main body after the grenadiers, and the Fifty-Fifth and Forty-Second Highlanders in reserve. It was little that they could see through the tangle of fallen trees and dying leaves; possibly they caught a glimpse of the top of the breastwork but of not a white coat of the defenders behind it.

On they came in full confidence, knowing nothing of the obstacles before them, when suddenly the breast-work broke into a sheet of flame and a storm of grape and musketry swept the ranks from end to end. Abercromby's instructions had been that the position should be taken with the bayonet, but all order was lost in the maze of fallen trees, and very soon the men began to return the fire as they advanced, but with little effect, for not an enemy could they see. Nevertheless, though riddled through and through, they scrambled on over the prostrate trunks straight upon the breastwork, when they were

stopped by the tangled hedge and sharpened boughs of the inner abatis. Strive as they might they could not force their way through this under the terrible fire that rained on them in front and flank from the angles of the breastwork; and after an hour's struggle they fell back, exclaiming that the position was impregnable. Reports were sent to Abercromby, who throughout the action had never moved from the saw-mills, two miles away, and for all answer there came back the simple order to attack again.

And then came such a scene as had not been witnessed since Malplaquet nor was to be seen again till Badajoz. The men stormed forward anew, furious with rage and heedless of bullets or grape-shot, through the network of trunks and boughs against their invisible enemy. Behind the breast-work the French were cheering loudly, hoisting their hats occasionally above the parapet and laughing when they were blown to pieces, but pouring in always a deadly and unquenchable fire; while the British struggled on, grimed with sweat and smoke, vowing that they would have that wooden wall at any cost. The Highlanders broke loose from the reserve with claymores drawn and slashed their way through the branches to the breast-work, and the British rushed after them to its foot but could advance no further. They had no ladders, and as fast as they hoisted one another to the top of the breast-work they were shot down.

Montcalm, cool and collected, moved to and fro among his men in his shirt-sleeves, always at the point of greatest danger, to cheer them and keep them to the fight. The French fire was appalling in its destruction. Men who had passed through the ordeal of Fontenoy declared that it was child's play compared with Ticonderoga. Nevertheless not once only, but thrice more, the British and the Americans with them hurled themselves desperately against the French stronghold, only to be beaten back time after time, until the inner abatis was hung with wisps of scarlet, like poppies that grow through a hedge of thorn, some swaying with the contortions that told of living agony, some limp and still in the merciful stillness of death. The fight had endured for five hours, when some officer of more intelligence than his fellows formed two columns and made a fifth attack upon the extreme right of the French position. The men hewed their way to the breast-work, and for a time the fate of this unequal day hung trembling in the balance.

Montcalm hurried to the threatened quarter with his reserves, but only by desperate exertion held his own, for the Highlanders fought with a fury that would yield neither to discipline nor to death. Captain John Campbell and a few of his men actually scaled the wooden wall and dropped down within it, but only to be pierced at once by a score of bayonets. Finally at six o'clock a last attack was delivered, as heroic, as hopeless, and as fruitless as the rest; and then the order was given to retreat. The Highlanders were with the greatest difficulty forced away from their fallen comrades, and under cover of the skirmishers' fire the British withdrew, shattered, exhausted, and demoralised.

And then came one of those strange and dreadful scenes which break an officer's heart. Hardly was the retreat sounded when the very men who for six hours had faced the mouth of hell without flinching were seized with panic and fled in wild disorder through forest and swamp to the landing-place, leaving their arms, their accoutrements, the very shoes from their feet to mark the track of their flight. Fortunately Bradstreet and his armed boatmen mounted guard over the boats and prevented the fugitives from setting themselves afloat. Abercromby came up, as abject as the worst, despatched orders for the wounded and the heavy artillery to be sent back to New York, and followed himself so speedily with his humiliated troops that he arrived at the head of Lake George before his messenger. There he entrenched himself and sat still, while the reckoning of his ignorance and folly was made up.

Of the Provincial troops three hundred and thirty-four had fallen before Ticonderoga; of the seven British battalions no fewer than sixteen hundred. The Forty-Second lost close on five hundred men and officers killed and wounded, the Forty-Fourth and Forty-Sixth each about two hundred, the Fifty-Fifth and the fourth battalion of the Sixtieth each about one hundred and fifty, the Twenty-Seventh and first battalion of the Sixtieth each about a hundred. The loss of the French was less than three hundred and fifty, and Montcalm might well praise his gallant soldiers and hug himself over his victory, for he had fended off attack on Canada for at least one year.

The French general contented himself with strengthening the defences of Ticonderoga and sending out parties of irregulars to harass Abercromby's communications with Fort Edward. Abercromby for his part remained throughout July and the first days of August glued to his camp at the head of Lake George, losing many men from dysentery but attempting nothing.

CHAPTER 12

The Attack on Duquêsne

At last Abercromby made over to Bradstreet a force of twenty-five hundred men, Provincial troops for the most part, and sent him to attack the French post of Fort Frontenac, which guarded the outlet of Lake Ontario into the St. Lawrence. The project was Bradstreet's own and had been favourably regarded some time before by Loudoun; but it was only under pressure of a council of war that Abercromby's assent to it was wrung from him.

Bradstreet accordingly dropped down to Albany, and advanced by the Mohawk and Onandaga to the site of Oswego, where he launched out on to the lake on the 22nd of August, and on the 25th landed safely near Fort Frontenac. The French garrison being little over one hundred strong could make small resistance, and on the 27th surrendered as prisoners of war, leaving nine vessels, which constituted the entire naval force of the French on the lake, in Bradstreet's hands. The fort was dismantled, two of the ships were carried off, the remainder were burned since there was no fort at Oswego to protect them, and Bradstreet returned triumphant to Albany. The service that he had rendered was of vast importance. The command of Lake Ontario was lost to the French, their communications north and south were severed, the alliance of a number of wavering Indian tribes was secured for the British, and Fort Duquêsne, the point against which Pitt had levelled his third blow, was left isolated and alone.

Heartened by this success and by the news of Louisburg, Abercromby began to write vaguely of a second attempt upon Ticonderoga as soon as Amherst should have reinforced him; but it was October before the conqueror of Louisburg reached Lake George, and then both commanders agreed that the season was too far spent for further operations. The troops were accordingly sent into winter quarters, and

Canada was [1] saved for another year. It now remains to be seen how matters fared with Brigadier Forbes at Fort Duquêsne.

Forbes himself had arrived at Philadelphia early in April, to find that no army was ready for him. The Provincial troops allotted to him from Pennsylvania, Virginia, Maryland, and North Carolina had not even been enlisted; Montgomery's Highlanders were in the south, and only half of Colonel Bouquet's battalion of the Sixtieth was within reach. It was the end of June before the various fractions of his force were on march: and meanwhile the general was seized with a dangerous and agonising internal disease, against which he fought with a courage and resolution which was as admirable as it was pathetic. Forbes's career had been somewhat singular. He hailed from county Fife and had begun life as a medical student, but had entered the Scots Greys as a cornet and had risen to command the regiment. He had served in Flanders and Germany on the staff of Stair, Ligonier, and General Campbell, and finally as Cumberland's quartermaster-general. [2]

But though all his training had been in the old formal school he had recognised, as has been seen, that in America he must learn a new art of war. He had studied Braddock's failure, and had perceived that even if Braddock had succeeded he must inevitably have retired from Fort Duquêsne from want of supplies. Instead, therefore, of making one long march with an unmanageable train of waggons, he decided to advance by short stages, establishing fortified magazines at every forty miles, and at last, when within reach of his destination, to march upon it with his entire force and with as few encumbrances as possible. This plan he had learned from a French treatise, [3] though he might have gathered it from a study of Monk's campaign in the Highlands had the opportunity been open to him. Nor was Bouquet, a Swiss by nationality, less assiduous in thinking out new methods.

His views as to equipment have already been noticed; but knowing the value of marksmanship in the woods, Bouquet obtained a certain number of rifled carbines for his own battalion, and thus turned a part of the Sixtieth into Riflemen before their time. [4] He also introduced a new system of drill for work in the forest, forming his men into small columns of two abreast which could deploy into line in two minutes.

---

1. Abercromby to Pitt, 8th September 1758

2. Stewart's *Highlanders*, vol. i.

3. Turpin's *Essai sur la guerre*. Forbes to Pitt, 17th June, 27th October 1758.

4. *Add. MS.*, 21643. Receipt for the rifles, 6th May; Stanwix to Bouquet, 25th May 1758.

Under such commanders the mistakes of Braddock were not likely to be repeated. [5]

Then came the question whether Braddock's route should be followed, or a new but shorter line of advance from Pennsylvania. Virginia was furiously jealous lest Pennsylvania should reap the advantage of a direct road to the trading station on the Ohio, and Washington was urgent in recommending the old road; but Forbes had no respect for provincial squabbles and decided for Pennsylvania. He had much difficulty in shaping the Provincials into soldiers, the material delivered to him being of the rawest, and destitute of the remotest idea of discipline. It was not till the beginning of July that Bouquet with an advanced party encamped at Raystown, now the town of Bedford, on the eastern slope of the Alleghanies, and that Forbes was able to move to the frontier village of Carlisle and thence to Shippensburg. There his illness increased, with pain so excruciating that he was unable to advance farther until September. Bouquet meanwhile pushed forward the construction of a road over the Alleghanies with immense labour and under prodigious difficulties. The wildness and desolation of the country seems somewhat to have awed even the stern resolution of Forbes. He wrote to Pitt:

> It is an immense uninhabited wilderness, overgrown everywhere with trees or brushwood, so that nowhere can one see twenty yards.

Through this with its endless obstacles of jungle, ravine, and swamp Bouquet's men worked their way. The first fortified magazine had been made at Raystown and named Fort Bedford; the next was to be on the western side of the main river Alleghany at a stream called Loyalhannon Creek. Progress was necessarily slow, but Forbes's advance was not made so leisurely without an object. The French had collected a certain number of Indians for the defence of Fort Duquêsne; but if the attack were delayed it was tolerably certain that these fickle and unstable allies would grow tired of waiting and disperse to their homes. Forbes meanwhile lost no opportunity of conciliating these natives; and by the efforts of his emissaries the most powerful tribes were persuaded to join the side of the British, and scornfully to reject the rival overtures of the French.

But at this critical time a rash exploit of one of Bouquet's offic-

---

5. *Ibid.*, 21632. Bouquet to Forbes, 20th August 1758.

ers went near to wreck the whole enterprise. Major Grant of the Highlanders entreated permission to go forward with a small party to reconnoitre Fort Duquêsne, capture a few prisoners, and strike some blow which might discourage and weaken the French. Eight hundred men of the Highlanders, Sixtieth, and Provincial troops were accordingly made over to him; so setting out with these from Loyalhannon he arrived before dawn of the 14th of September at a hill, since named Grant's hill, within half a mile of the fort. With incredible rashness he scattered his force in all directions. Leaving a fourth of his men to guard the baggage, he sent parties out to right and left, took post himself two miles in advance of the baggage with a hundred men, and sent an officer forward with a company of Highlanders into the open plain to draw a map of the fort.

Finally, as if to call attention to his own folly, he ordered reveille to be beaten with all possible parade. The French and Indians at once swarmed out of the fort and drove all the parties back in confusion upon one another. The Highlanders were seized with panic at the yells of the Indians and took to their heels, and but for the firmness of the Virginians of the baggage-guard the whole force would probably have been cut to pieces. As it was, nearly three hundred men were killed, wounded, or taken, and Grant himself was among the prisoners. Forbes, who amid all torments, troubles, and reverses preserved always a keen sense of the ridiculous, declared that he could make nothing of the affair except that his friend Grant had lost his wits; which indeed was a concise and accurate summary of the whole proceeding.

But such paltry success could avail the French little, for Bradstreet's capture of Fort Frontenac had already decided the fate of Fort Duquêsne. The French commander, his supplies being cut off, was obliged to dismiss the greater number of his men; otherwise Forbes could hardly have penetrated to the Ohio in that year. The elements fought for the French. Heavy rain ruined Bouquet's new road; the horses being underfed and overworked kept breaking down fast; the magazines at Raystown and Loyalhannon were emptied faster than they could be replenished; and Forbes was in despair. All through October the rain continued until at length it gave place to snow, and the roads became a sea of mud over which retreat and advance were alike impossible. At the beginning of November the General, though now sick unto death, was carried to Loyalhannon, where he decided that no attack could be attempted for that season.

Intelligence, however, was brought that the French were so weak in numbers as to be defenceless; and on the 18th, twenty-five hundred picked men marched off without tents or baggage, Forbes himself travelling in a litter at their head. At midnight of the 24th the sentries heard the sound of a distant explosion, and on the next day at dusk the troops reached the blackened ruins of what had been Fort Duquêsne. The fortifications had been blown up; barracks and store-houses were in ashes; there was no sign of anything human except the heads of the Highlanders who had been killed in Grant's engagement, stuck up on poles with their kilts hung in derision round them.

Their Highland comrades went mad with rage at the sight; but the French and their allies were gone, having evacuated and destroyed the fort and retired to the fort of Venango farther up the Alleghany river. Forbes planted a stockade around a cluster of huts that were still undestroyed, and named it Pittsburg in honour of the minister. Arrangements were then made for leaving a garrison of two hundred Provincials to hold the post, for there could be no doubt that the French would collect a force from Venango and Niagara to endeavour to retake it. The garrison indeed was far too small, but there was not food enough for more; so this handful of poor men was left perforce to make the best of its solitude during the dreary days of the winter.

One duty still remained to be done before Forbes's column turned homeward,—to search for the bones of those who had fallen with Braddock. A party of Pennsylvanians made their way through the forest to the Monongahela, Major Halket of Forbes's staff accompanying them. Among the multitude of ghastly relics two skeletons were found lying together under one tree. Halket recognised the one by a peculiarity of the teeth as that of his father, Sir Peter Halket of the Forty-Fourth; and in the other he thought that he saw his brother, who had fallen by his side. The two were wrapped in a Highlander's plaid and buried in one grave, under a volley fired by the Pennsylvanians. The rest of the remains were buried together in one deep trench; and then at the beginning of December the troops marched back to Pennsylvania with the dying Forbes in their midst.

With great difficulty the general was brought still living to Philadelphia, where he lingered on through the winter and died in the following March. Though no brilliant action marked his advance to the Ohio he had accomplished his work against endless difficulties and in extremity of bodily torture; and that work was the taking from France of half of her Indian allies, the relief of the western border from Pennsylvania to Maryland from Indian raids, and the opening to the

British of the vast regions of the West.

So ended the American campaign of 1758. The French had been struck hard on both flanks, at Louisburg in the north and on the Ohio in the south, but in the centre they had held their own. Two parts out of three of Pitt's design had been accomplished; but the most important success of all was that achieved by Bradstreet in severing the French communications at Fort Frontenac. It may be that Pitt thought best to adhere to the plan of operations mapped out for him by Loudoun, or it may be that he wished to retrieve the reputation lost by Braddock's defeat; but the fact remains that he meditated no attack on Niagara or Fort Frontenac, the capture of either of which would have entailed that of Fort Duquêsne, and that despite the industry of Bouquet and the tenacity of Forbes the advance to the Ohio would have been impossible but for the brilliant and successful enterprise of Bradstreet.

Map of operations of the french & Indian war

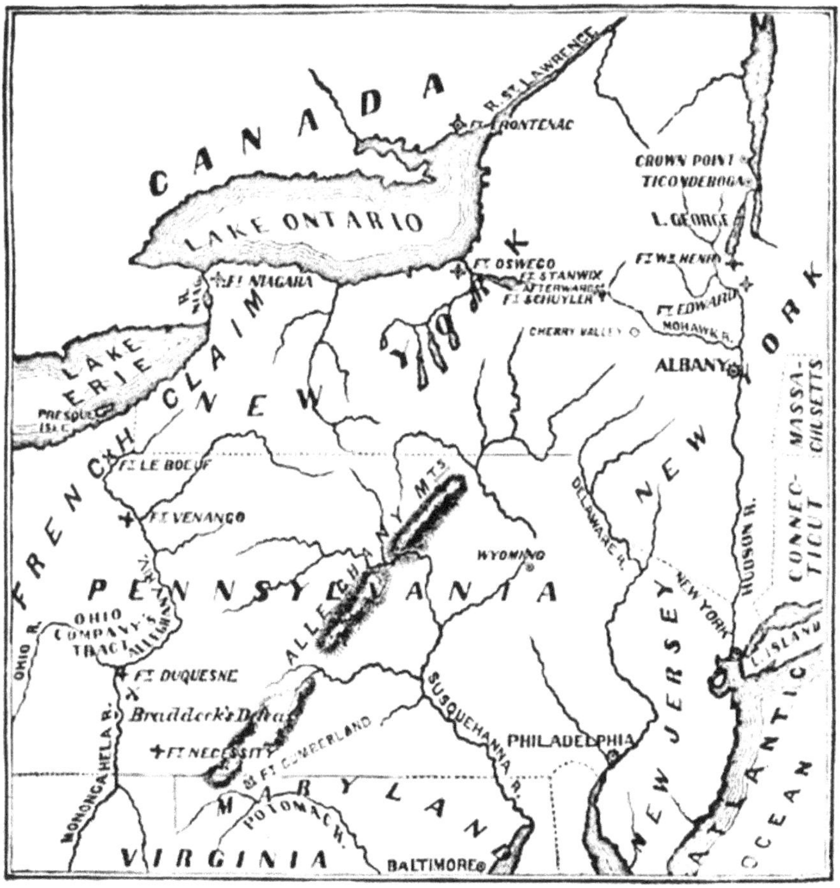

CHAPTER 13

Wolfe & Quebec

It was late in November 1758, before Parliament reassembled, and listened to a speech from the throne, jubilant over the captures of Louisburg, Fort Frontenac, and Senegal, but modestly deploring the inevitable expense of the war. The Commons, however, were practically unanimous in allowing a free hand to Pitt, though the minister himself was startled when he was brought face to face with the estimates. Those for the army were introduced a week later, and showed but a slight increase in the British Establishment, the total number of men not exceeding eighty-five thousand. Yet the main operations of the coming year were to be conducted on a grander scale than before, while at the same time provision was needed to make good the enormous waste caused by tropical expeditions. Two new regiments only were formed before the actual opening of the operations of 1759, one of them, Colonel Eyre Coote's, [1] serving as a reminder that concurrently with all other enterprises there was progressing the struggle for the mastery of the East Indies.

Pitt's principal effort, as in the previous year, was directed against Canada, and the operations prescribed were little less complicated than those of the last campaign. In the first place a direct attack was to be made upon Quebec, for which purpose Amherst was to make over ten battalions to General Wolfe. In 1759. the second, the attempt to penetrate into Canada by way of Ticonderoga and Crown Point was to be renewed. Amherst himself was to take this duty upon him, Abercromby having been rightly recalled; and it was hoped that he might join Wolfe in the capital of Canada or at least make a powerful diversion in his favour. At the same time Amherst was ordered to se-

1. Coote's, which took rank as the 84th, was raised by order of 10th January 1759. Sebright's, raised in Ireland 14th October 1758, was numbered the 83rd.

cure Oswego and Pittsburg, and empowered to undertake any further operations that he pleased, without prejudice to the main objects of the campaign. The general having already twenty-three battalions of the king's troops in America, it was reckoned that, with the regiments to be forwarded to him from the West Indies by Hopson, he would possess a sufficient force for the work. No fresh battalions therefore were sent to him from England. [2]

The selection of James Wolfe for the command of the expedition against Quebec came as a surprise to many. He was now thirty-two years of age, and had held a commission ever since he was fourteen, attaining the rank of captain at seventeen and of major at twenty. He had served in Flanders and distinguished himself as brigade-major at Lauffeld, but it was as lieutenant-colonel in command of the Twentieth Foot that he had shown himself most competent. He was an admirable regimental officer, enthusiastic over his profession and well acquainted with its duties, a stern disciplinarian yet devoted to his men, and a re-fined and educated gentleman. In short he was a commanding officer who could be trusted to raise the tone of any corps. [3] He had attracted Pitt's notice by his constant though fruitless advocacy of action in the abortive descent on Rochefort in 1757, and had come prominently before the public eye by his behaviour at Louisburg.

His relations with Amherst, however, appear not to have been very friendly, nor to have been improved by his return home from Cape Breton in 1758; indeed Wolfe was reprimanded as soon as he arrived in England for returning without the king's orders, under misconception of his letter of service. [4] It was possibly under the sting of this censure that he wrote to Pitt declaring his readiness to serve in America and "particularly in the river St. Lawrence"; but be that as it may he received the appointment. There is an anecdote that he filled the great minister with dismay by some extraordinary *gasconnade* at a dinner to which he had been invited shortly before his departure; but even if, in a moment of elation, [5] he may have given way to excited talk for a time, yet such outbursts were not usual with him, for he was the qui-etest and most modest of men. The real objection to his appointment

<hr>

2. Pitt to Amherst, 29th December 1758; 23rd January, 10th March 1759.
3. See his *Regimental Orders*, 1749-1755, collected in a little volume. My own copy is the 2nd edition, 1780.
4. *Secretary's Common Letter Book*, 2nd October 1758.
5. Lord Temple, who is the authority for the story, was careful to mention that Wolfe was perfectly sober.

was the state of his health. He had never been strong and was a martyr to rheumatism and stone, but he was as courageous against pain as against the bullets of the enemy; in fact, like King William the Third, he was never so happy as when under fire.

For the rest nature had cursed him with a countenance of singular ugliness, his portraits showing a profile that runs in a ridiculous curve from the forehead to the tip of the nose, and recedes in as ridiculous a curve from the nose to the neck. A shock of red hair tied in a queue, and a tall, lank, ungainly figure added neither grace nor beauty to his appearance; but within that unhandsome frame lay a passionate attachment to the British soldier, and an indomitable spirit against difficulty and danger.

It was the middle of February when Wolfe sailed from England in H.M.S. *Neptune*, the flag-ship of a fleet of twenty-one sail under Admirals Saunders, Holmes, and Durell. The voyage was long and tedious, and when at last Louisburg was reached the harbour was found to be blocked with ice, so that the fleet was obliged to make for Halifax. From thence Durell was detached, too late as was presently proved, to the mouth of the St. Lawrence to intercept certain transports that were expected with supplies from France; Holmes was sent to convoy the troops that were to sail from New York; and in May the entire armament for the reduction of Quebec was assembled at Louisburg.

Wolfe had been led to expect a force of twelve thousand men; but the regiments which should have been detached from Guadeloupe could not yet be spared, and those drawn from the garrisons of Nova Scotia had been reduced considerably beneath their proper strength by sickness during the winter. The quality of the troops, however, was excellent, and on this Wolfe counted to make good a serious numerical deficiency. The force was distributed into three brigades, under Brigadiers Monckton, Townsend, and Murray, all three of them men of youth, energy, and talent, well qualified to serve under such a commander as Wolfe. [6]

The grenadiers of the army were, as had now become usual, massed together and organised in two divisions, those of the regiments in garrison at Louisburg being known as the Louisburg grenadiers. [7] Another separate corps was composed of the best marksmen in the

---

6. The distribution was as follows: Monckton's brigade, 15th, 43rd, 58th, Fraser's Highlanders. Townsend's brigade, 28th, 47th, 2/60th. Murray's Brigade, 35th, 48th, 3/60th.

7. These regiments were the 22nd, 40th, and 45th.

several regiments, and was called the Light Infantry, while six companies of Provincial rangers furnished a proportion of irregular troops. The whole strength of the force was thus brought up to about eight thousand five hundred men. A fortnight sufficed for the final arrangements, for Amherst and his staff had spared no pains to provide all that was necessary; [8] and on the 6th of June the last division of transports, amid a roar of cheering from the men, sailed out of Louisburg for the St. Lawrence.

The French commanders meanwhile had been anxiously making their preparations for defence. There could be no doubt that the British would make at least a double attack upon Canada, from Lake Champlain on the south and Lake Ontario on the west, and every able-bodied man in the colony was called out to repel it. No sooner had the dispositions been settled than news came of the intended advance by the St. Lawrence, which threw the whole colony into consternation. Five regular battalions and the militia from every part of Canada were summoned, together with a thousand Indians, to Quebec; and after much debate Montcalm, who held the command of the troops under the governor of the city, decided on his scheme of defence.

Quebec with its fortifications stands on the north bank of the St. Lawrence, being situated on a rocky headland which marks the contraction of the river from a width of fifteen or twenty miles to a strait scarcely exceeding one. Immediately to northward of this ridge the river St. Charles flows down to the St. Lawrence; and seven miles to eastward of the St. Charles the shore is cut by the rocky gorge through which pours the cataract of the Montmorenci. It was between these two streams that Montcalm disposed his army, his right resting on the St. Charles, his left on the Montmorenci, with his headquarters on the little river of Beauport midway between the two, and his front to the St. Lawrence.

All along the border of the great river were thrown up entrenchments, batteries, and redoubts. From Montmorenci to Beauport abrupt and rocky heights raised these defences too high above the water to be reached by the cannon of ships. From Beauport to the St. Charles stretched broad flats of mud, which were commanded by batteries both afloat and ashore, as well as by the guns of Quebec. On the walls of the city itself were mounted over one hundred cannon; a bridge of boats with a strong bridge-head on the eastern side preserved the

8. Wolfe to Pitt, 6th June 1759.

communication between city and camp; and for the defence of the river itself there was a floating battery of twelve heavy guns besides several gun-boats and fire-ships. The vessels of the convoy that Durell had failed to intercept, together with the frigates that escorted them, were sent up the river beyond Quebec to be out of harm's way; and the sailors were taken to man the batteries ashore. Thus strongly entrenched with fourteen thousand men of one description and another, and firm in the belief that no foreign ship would dare to attempt the intricate navigation of the St. Lawrence, Montcalm waited for the British to come.

It was not until the 21st of June that the first mast-heads of the fleet were seen. For days the British had been groping their way up the river, helped partly by a captured Canadian pilot, more often by their own skill and experience. "Damn me if there are not a thousand places in the Thames fifty times more hazardous than this," growled an old skipper on one of the transports, as he waived the pilot contemptuously aside. So the great fleet crept up the stream, ships of the line passing where the French had feared to take a coasting schooner, and at last on the 26th of June the whole was anchored safely off the southern shore of the Isle of Orleans, a few miles below Quebec. No single mishap had marred this masterly and superb feat of pilotage.

The troops landed without resistance next day on the Isle of Orleans, and on the same afternoon a sudden squall drove many of the ships ashore and destroyed several of the flat-boats prepared for the disembarkation. The storm raised high hopes of providential deliverance in the French, which, however, were speedily dashed, for the tempest subsided as suddenly as it had arisen. On the morrow therefore the Governor of Quebec resolved to launch his fire-ships down the river upon the fleet. The attempt was duly made, but the ships were ill-handled and the service ill-executed. The British sailors coolly rowed out, grappled the burning vessels and towed them ashore, while the troops, formed up in order of battle, gazed at the most imposing display of fireworks that they had ever seen.

Meanwhile Wolfe reconnoitred the French lines and the city, but could see no possible opening for a successful attack. One thing alone seemed feasible, to occupy the heights of Point Lévis over against Quebec on the southern shore, and to fire across this, the narrowest part of the river, upon the city. Monckton's brigade accordingly entrenched itself on these heights, threw up batteries, and on the 12th of July opened a fire which wrought havoc among the buildings of

Quebec. But however this cannonade might afflict the nerves of the inhabitants, it could contribute little, as Wolfe well knew, to advance the real work in hand.

Accordingly, while the batteries on Point Lévis were constructing, the English general resolved to see whether a vulnerable point could be found on Montcalm's left flank. On the 8th of July, leaving a detachment to hold the camp on the Isle of Orleans, he sent Townsend's and Murray's brigades across to the northern bank of the St. Lawrence, where they proceeded to entrench themselves on the eastern side of the Montmorenci. The movement was highly perilous, since it divided his force into three portions, no one of which could support the other; but the French kept themselves rigidly on the defensive, though the British lay but a gunshot from them across the rocky gorge of the Montmorenci and annoyed their camp not a little with their artillery. Still Wolfe could accomplish nothing decisive. The news that Amherst was advancing against Ticonderoga did indeed discourage the Canadians and increase desertion among them; but in all other respects the operations before Quebec had come to a deadlock.

Now, however, the fleet which had already vanquished the difficulties in the navigation of the St. Lawrence once more came forward to show the way. It was the opinion of the French that no vessel could pass the batteries of Quebec without destruction; but on the night of the 18th of July H.M.S. *Sutherland*, of fifty guns, with several smaller vessels, sailed safely up the river, covered by the fire of the guns on Point Lévis, destroyed some small craft which they found there and anchored above the town.

This was the first menace of an attempt to take Quebec in reverse, and obliged Montcalm to detach six hundred men from the camp of Beauport to defend the few accessible points between the city and Cap Rouge, some eight miles above it. Wolfe took advantage of the movement also to send a detachment to ravage the country to westward of Quebec; but though he thus added a fourth to the three isolated divisions into which he had broken up his army, Montcalm still declined to move. A second attempt July 28. was indeed made to destroy the British vessels by fireships, which was frustrated like the first by the coolness and gallantry of the British sailors; but beyond this French aggression would not go. Montcalm was resolved to play the part of Fabius, and he seemed likely to play it with success.

The season was now wearing on, and Wolfe was not a whit nearer to his object than at his first disembarkation. Mortified by his ill-suc-

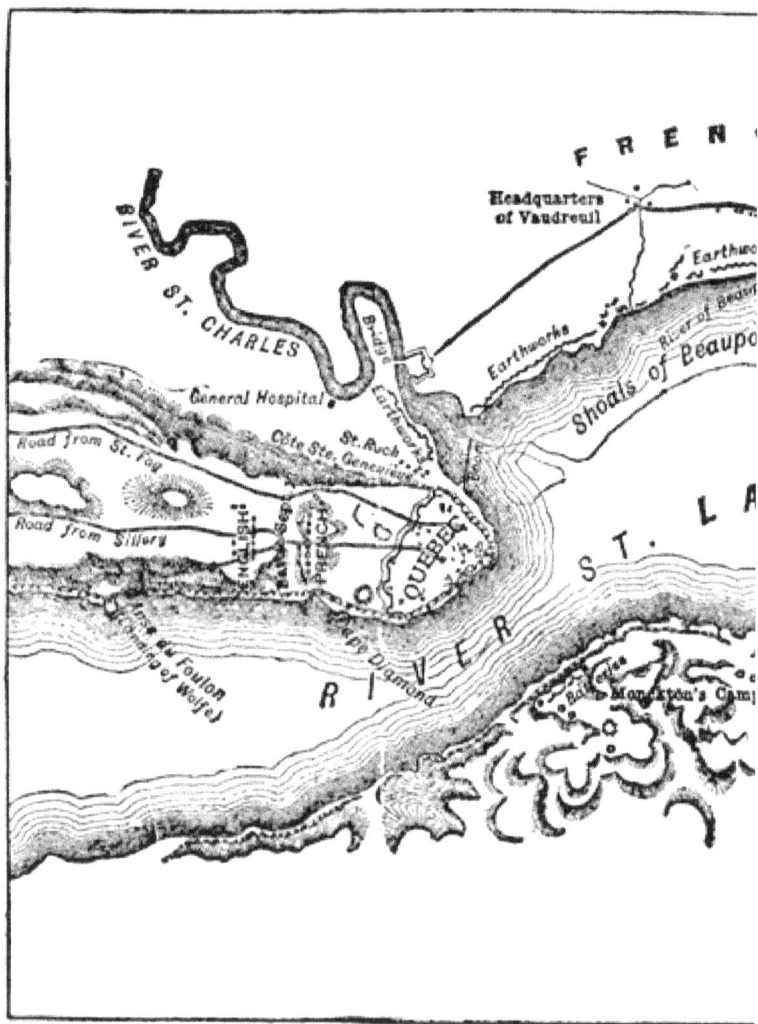

FREN...

Headquarters
of Vaudreuil

Earthwo...

River of Beau...

Earthworks

Shoals of Beaupo...

Bridge

RIVER ST. CHARLES

General Hospital

Earthwor...

St. Roch

Road from St. Foy

Côte Ste. Genevieve

Road from Sillery

ENGLISH

FRENCH

QUEBEC

RIVER ST. LA...

Cape Diamond

Cove and Foulon
(Landing of Wolfe)

RIVER ST. LA...

Monckton's Camp

Scale of Miles

C H
C A M P

"Headquarters of Montcalm

Headquarters of Levis

Falls of Montmorenci

Wolfe's Camp

Earthworks

Earthworks

orks

Floating Battery

Shoals

Black Rock

rt

W R E N C E

Point Levy

Point of Orleans

Hardy's Camp

ISLAND OF ORLEANS

SIEGE OF QUEBEC
1759.

cess he now resolved to attack Montcalm's camp in front. The hazard was desperate, for, after leaving troops to hold Point Lévis and the entrenchments on the Montmorenci, he could raise little more than five thousand men with which to attack a force of more than double his strength in a very formidable position. A mile to westward of the falls of the Montmorenci there is a strand about a furlong wide at high water and half a mile wide at low tide, between that river and the foot of the cliffs.

The French had built redoubts on this strand above highwater mark, which were commanded, though Wolfe could not see it, by the fire of musketry from the entrenchments above. Wolfe's hope was that by the capture of one of these redoubts he might tempt the French down to regain it and so bring on a general action, or at least find an opportunity of reconnoitring the entrenched camp itself. Moreover, below the falls of the Montmorenci was a ford, by which some at least of his troops on that river could join in the attack, and so diminish in some degree the disparity of numbers. But Wolfe held the Canadian militia in such contempt that he was not afraid to pit against them, at whatever odds, the valour of his own disciplined soldiers.

Accordingly on the morning of the 31st of July H.M.S. *Centurion* stood in close to the Montmorenci, dropped her anchor and opened fire on the redoubts. Two armed transports followed her and likewise opened fire on the nearest redoubt, stranding as the tide ebbed till at last they lay high and dry on the mud. Simultaneously the batteries on the other side of the Montmorenci opened a furious fire upon the flank of Montcalm's entrenchments, and at eleven o'clock a number of boats filled with troops rowed across from Point Lévis and hovered about the river opposite Beauport as if to attack at that point. Time, however, showed Montcalm where real danger was to be apprehended, and he concentrated the whole of his twelve thousand men between Beauport and the Montmorenci.

At half-past five the British batteries afloat and ashore opened fire with redoubled fury, and the boats made a dash for the shore. Unfortunately some of them grounded on a ledge short of the flats, which caused some confusion and delay, but eventually all of them reached the strand and set the men ashore. Thirteen companies of grenadiers were the first to land, and after them two hundred men of the Sixtieth; while some distance behind them the Fifteenth and Fraser's Highlanders followed in support. No sooner were they ashore than the grenadiers, the most trusted troops in the army, for some reason got out of hand. Despite the efforts of their officers they would not wait for the supports to form up, but made a rush in the greatest disorder and confusion for the redoubt and drove the French from it. Instantly a tremendous fire was poured upon them from the entrenchments above.

The grenadiers recoiled for a moment; then recovering themselves they ran forward again and made a mad effort to struggle up the steep, slippery grass of the ascent, but only to roll down by scores, killed or wounded by the hail of musketry from the French lines. Where the affair would have ended it is hard to say, had not the clouds of a summer's storm, which had hung over the river all the afternoon, suddenly burst just at that moment in a deluge of rain. All ammunition on both sides was drenched, so that further firing became impossible, while the grassy slope became so treacherous that it was hopeless to attempt to climb it. Wolfe, seeing that everything was gone wrong, ordered a retreat; and the troops fell back and re-embarked, the grenadiers and Sixtieth having lost five hundred officers and men, or well-nigh half of their numbers, in killed, wounded, and missing.

Wolfe was highly indignant over the misbehaviour of the grenadiers, and rebuked them sharply in general orders for their impetuous, irregular, and unsoldierlike proceedings. The French, on the other hand, were naturally much elated, and flattered themselves that the campaign was virtually at an end. Nor was Wolfe of a very different opinion. It is said, indeed, that he conceived the idea of leaving a part of his troops in a fortified position before Quebec, to be ready for a new attempt in the following spring.

Meanwhile for the present he fell back on the tactics, which Barrington had so successfully employed at Guadeloupe, of laying waste all the settlements round about Quebec, with the object of provoking desertion among the militia and exhausting the colony generally. Montcalm, however, was not to be enticed from his lines; he had Indians with him sufficient to make hideous reprisals for Wolfe's desolation, and Canada was not to be won by the burning of villages. Wolfe, therefore, now shifted his operations to the point whither the enterprise of the fleet had led him, above and on the reverse side of Quebec. With every fair wind more and more ships had braved the fire of the batteries and passed through August 5. it in safety; and now a flotilla of flat-boats dared the same passage, while twelve hundred men under Brigadier Murray marched overland up the south bank of the St. Lawrence to do service in them.

This movement compelled Montcalm to withdraw another fifteen hundred men from the camp at Beauport, to check any attempt at a landing above the city. The duty thus imposed upon this small body of French was most arduous, since it involved anxious watching of fifteen or twenty miles of the shore. So well was it performed, however, under the direction of Bougainville, an officer afterwards famous as the great navigator, that it was only after two repulses that Murray succeeded in burning a large magazine of French stores. The alarm caused by this stroke was so great that Montcalm hastened from Beauport to take command in person; but when he arrived the British had already retired, content with their success.

None the less the French from the highest to the lowest now grew seriously uneasy. Their army was on short rations. All its supplies were drawn from the districts of Three Rivers and Montreal; and, from want of transport overland, these were perforce sent down the river where the British ships lay ready to intercept them.

Now was seen the error of sending the frigates up the river and allowing the British squadron to assemble by small detachments above Quebec; but it was too late to repair it. The British fleet had discovered the true method of reducing the city by severing its communications both above and below. The only hope for the French was that winter might drive the shipping from the St. Lawrence and put an end to the campaign, before Quebec should be starved out.

CHAPTER 14

Amherst's Advance

Meanwhile Amherst's operations to south and west began likewise to tell upon the situation. Taking advantage of the latitude allowed to him by Pitt, he determined to add the reduction of Niagara to the enterprises prescribed to him. This duty he assigned to Brigadier Prideaux with five thousand men; [1] Brigadier Stanwix was entrusted with the relief of Pittsburg; and Amherst in person took charge of the grand advance by Lakes George and Champlain. The operations of Prideaux and Stanwix were to be conducted in combination; for it was intended that while Prideaux was engaged with Niagara, Stanwix should push a force northward against the French posts on Lake Erie, and thence on to Niagara itself, thus releasing Prideaux for an advance to the St. Lawrence.

Prideaux was the first to take the field. His force having been assembled on the Mohawk at Senectady, he moved up the stream, left a strong garrison at Fort Stanwix to guard the Great Carrying-place, and moved forward by Lake Oneida and the River Onandaga to Oswego. There leaving nearly half of his force under Colonel Haldimand to secure his retreat, he embarked with the rest on the lake for Niagara. The fort stood in the angle formed by the river Niagara and Lake Ontario, and was garrisoned by some six hundred men. Prideaux at once laid siege in form, though the trenches were at first so unskilfully laid out by the engineers as to require almost total reconstruction. At last, however, the batteries opened fire. Prideaux was unluckily killed almost immediately by the premature explosion of a shell from one of his own guns, but Sir William Johnson, who had joined the force with a party of Indians, took command in his place and pushed the siege with great energy.

---

1. The 44th, 46th, 4/60th and 2500 New York Provincials. Amherst to Pitt, 7th May 1759.

SIR JEFFREY AMHERST

The fort after two or three weeks of battering was in extremity; when a party of thirteen hundred French rangers and Indians, which had been summoned from the work of harassing the British on the Ohio to the relief of Niagara, appeared on the scene in the very nick of time. Johnson rose worthily to the occasion. Leaving a third of his force in the trenches and yet another third to guard his boats, he sallied forth with the remainder to meet the relieving force, and after a brisk engagement routed it completely.

The survivors fled hurriedly back to Lake Erie, burned Venango and the posts on the lake and retired to Detroit. Niagara surrendered on the evening of the same day, and thus were accomplished at a stroke the most important objects to be gained by Stanwix and Prideaux. The whole region of the Upper Ohio was left in undisputed possession of the British, and the French posts of the West were hopelessly cut off from Canada. Now, therefore, the ground was open for an advance on Montreal by Lake Ontario; and Amherst lost no time in sending General Gage to take command of Prideaux's force, with orders to attack the French post of La Galette, at the head of the rapids of the St. Lawrence, and thence to push on as close as possible to Montreal. Amherst wrote to him:

Now is the time, and we must make use of it. [2]

Amherst himself had assembled his army at the end of June at the usual rendezvous by the head of Lake George. His force consisted of about eleven thousand five hundred men, five thousand of them Provincials and the remainder British. [3] As was now the rule, he had massed the grenadiers of the army into one corps, and had formed also a body of Light Infantry which he had equipped appropriately for its work. [4] It was not, however, until the 21st of July that the troops were embarked, and that a flotilla little less imposing than Abercromby's set sail with a fair wind over Lake George. It was drawn up in four columns, the light troops and Provincials on either flank, the regular troops in the right centre and the artillery and baggage

2. Amherst to Gage, 28th July 1759.
3. 1st Brigade, Colonel Forster, 27th, 55th, 1 batt. 1st; 2nd Brigade, Colonel Grant, 17th, Montgomery's Highlanders, 42nd Highlanders.
4. Amherst to Barrington, 10th August (*Bouquet Papers*, Add., MS. 21644, 22nd Feb. 1759). Amherst had also introduced a new exercise for all regiments (*Bouquet Papers*, 21644, 20th Jan 1759), but what it was I have been unable to discover; though it seems (*Haldimand Papers*, Add., MS. 21661, 3rd August 1760) that he formed the infantry sometimes in two ranks only, the rear-rank "locking up" to the front.

in the left centre. An advanced and a rear-guard in line covered the head and tail of the columns, and an armed sloop followed in rear of all. Before dark they had reached the Narrows, and at daybreak of the following morning the force disembarked and marched, meeting with little resistance, by the route of Abercromby's second advance to Ticonderoga.

The entrenchments which had foiled the British in the previous year had been reconstructed but were found to be deserted; Bourlamaque, the French commander, having withdrawn his garrison, some thirty-five hundred men only, into the fort. Amherst brought up his artillery to lay siege in form, but on the night of the 26th a loud explosion announced that the French had July 26. abandoned Ticonderoga and blown up the works. It was, however, but one bastion that had been destroyed, so Amherst at once repaired the damage and made preparations for advance on Crown Point. On the 1st August. of August he learned that Bourlamaque had abandoned this fortress also, and fallen back to the strong position of Isle aux Noix at the northern outlet of Lake Champlain.

Amherst was now brought to a standstill, for the French had four armed vessels on the lake, and it was necessary for him to build vessels likewise for the protection of the flotilla before he could advance farther. He at once set about this work, concurrently with the erection of a strong fort at Crown Point, but unfortunately he began too late. Amherst was above all a methodical man, whose principle was to make good each step gained before he attempted to move again. Possibly he had not anticipated so easy an advance to Crown Point, but, be that as it may, he had made no provision for advancing beyond it, and when at last, by the middle of September, his ships were ready, the season was too far advanced for further operations. He tried to stir up Gage to hasten to the attack on La Galette, but without success. In fact by the middle of August the campaign of the armies of the south and west was virtually closed.

CHAPTER 15

The Rising Path

For the moment the news of Amherst's advance to Crown Point caused great alarm in Quebec, and Montcalm felt himself obliged to send Lévis, one of his best officers, to superintend the defence of Montreal. Gradually, however, as Amherst's inaction was prolonged, the garrison regained confidence; and meanwhile deep discouragement fell on the British. On the 20th of August Wolfe, who was much exhausted by hard work, anxiety, and mortification, fell seriously ill and was compelled to delegate the conduct of operations to a council of his brigadiers. Several plans were propounded to them, all of which they rejected in favour of an attempt to gain a footing on the ridge above the city, cut off Montcalm's supplies from Montreal, and compel him to fight or surrender. The course was that which had been marked out by the fleet from the moment that the ships had passed above Quebec.

It was indeed both difficult and hazardous, but it was the only plan that promised any hope of success; and the success, if attained, would be final. Wolfe accepted it forthwith and without demur. The army had lost over eight hundred men killed and wounded since the beginning of operations, and had been weakened still more seriously by disease; but the general was driven to desperation by sickness and disappointment and was ready to undertake any enterprise that commended itself to his officers.

On the last day of August he was sufficiently recovered to go abroad once more, and on the 2nd of September he wrote to Pitt the story of his failure up to that day and of his resolutions for the future, all in a strain of dejection that sank almost to despair.

On the following day the troops were skilfully withdrawn without loss from the camp on the Montmorenci. On the night of the 4th a flotilla of flat-boats passed successfully above the town with the baggage and stores, and on the 5th seven battalions marched westward overland from Point Lévis and embarked, together with Wolfe himself, on Admiral Holmes' ships. Montcalm thereupon reinforced Bougainville to a strength of three thousand men and charged him to watch the movements of the fleet with the utmost vigilance. Bougainville's headquarters were at Cap Rouge, with detached fortified posts at Sillery, six miles down the river, at Samos yet farther down, and at Anse du Foulon, now called Wolfe's Cove, a mile and a half above Quebec. It was by this last that Wolfe, searching the heights for mile after mile with his telescope, perceived a narrow path running up the face of the precipice. From the path he turned his glass to the post above it, and seeing but ten or twelve tents concluded that the guard was not numerous and might be overpowered. There then was a way found for the ascent of the cliffs from the river: the next problem was how to turn the discovery to good account.

On the morning of 7th of September Holmes' squadron weighed anchor and sailed up to Cap Rouge. The French instantly turned out to man their entrenchments; and Wolfe, having kept them in suspense for a sufficient time, ordered the troops into the boats and directed them to row up and down as if in search of a landing-place. The succeeding days were employed in a series of similar feints, the ships drifting daily up to Cap Rouge with the flood tide and dropping down to Quebec with the ebb, till Bougainville, who followed every movement with increasing anxiety and bewilderment, fairly wore out his troops with incessant marching to and fro.

At last on the 12th of September Wolfe's opportunity presented itself. Two deserters came in from Bougainville's camp with intelligence that at next ebb-tide a convoy of provisions would pass down the river to Quebec. Wolfe sent orders to Colonel Burton, who was in command of the standing camps, that all the men which he could spare from them should march at nightfall along the southern bank of the river, and wait at a chosen place for embarkation. As night fell Admiral Saunders moved out of the basin of Orleans with the main fleet and ranged the ships along the length of the camp at Beauport. The boats were then lowered and manned by marines, sailors, and such few soldiers as had been left below Quebec, while the ships opened fire on the beach as if to clear it for a landing.

Montcalm, completely deceived, massed the whole of his troops at Beauport, and kept them under arms to repel the threatened attack. Meanwhile Holmes' squadron, with boats moored alongside the transports, lay quietly anchored off Cap Rouge, nor showed sign of life until late dusk, when seventeen hundred men [1] took their places in the boats and drifted with the tide for some little distance up the stream. Bougainville marked the movement and made no doubt that attack was designed upon his headquarters. Night fell, dark and moonless, and all was quiet.

Monsieur Vergor, who commanded the post at Anse du Foulon, gave leave to most of his guard of Canadians to go harvesting, and saw no reason why he should not himself go comfortably to bed. Bougainville remained on the alert, doubtless impatient for the tide to turn, which would carry the British away from his quarters and leave him in peace. He did not know that Wolfe was even then on board the flagship making his final arrangements for the morrow's battle, and that he had handed the portrait of his betrothed to Captain John Jervis[2] of H.M.S. *Porcupine*, to be returned to her in the event of his death.

At length at two o'clock in the morning the tide ebbed. Two lanterns rose flickering to the maintop shrouds of the Sutherland; Wolfe and his officers stepped into their boat, and with the whole flotilla astern of them dropped silently down the river. After a due interval the sloops and frigates followed, with the second division of troops on board; [3] and Bougainville with a sigh of relief resolved not to harass his men by a fruitless march after them. For full two hours the boats pursued their way, when the silence was broken by the challenge of a French sentry.

"France," answered a Highland officer who had learned the French tongue on foreign service.

"What regiment?" pursued the sentry.

"The Queen's" (*de la Reine*) replied the officer, naming a corps that formed part of Bougainville's force.

The sentry, knowing that a convoy of provisions was expected, allowed the boats to pass; for though Bougainville had, as a matter of fact, countermanded the convoy, the guards had not been apprised of the countermand. Off Samos another sentry, visible not a pistol-shot away from the boats, again challenged.

1. 28th (300 men), 43rd, Howe's division of Light Infantry, 47th, 58th, 200 Highlanders.
2. Afterwards Lord St. Vincent.
3. 300 of the 15th, 240 grenadiers, 250 Highlanders, 200 Light Infantry, 400 of the 35th, 400 of the 60th. Total 1910.

"Provision-boats," answered the same officer, "don't make a noise or the English will hear."

Once more the boats were suffered to pass. Presently they rounded the headland of Anse du Foulon, and there no sentry was to be seen. The leading boats were carried by the current somewhat below the intended landing-place, and the troops disembarked below the path, on a narrow strand at the foot of the heights. Then twenty-four men of the Light Infantry, who had volunteered for a certain unknown but dangerous service under Colonel Howe, slung their muskets about them, threw themselves upon the face of the cliff, and began to drag themselves through the two hundred feet of stunted bush that separated them from the enemy.

The dawn was just breaking as they reached the top, and through the dim light they could distinguish the group of tents that composed Vergor's encampment. Instantly they dashed at them; and the French, utterly surprised, at once took to their heels. Vergor, who was reputed a coward, stood firm and fired his pistols; and the report of three of the British muskets, together with the cheers of Howe's forlorn hope, gave Wolfe the signal for which he waited. He uttered the word to advance, and the rest of the troops swarmed up the cliff to their comrades as best they could. The zigzag path which had first attracted Wolfe's eye was found to be obstructed by trenches and abatis, but these obstacles were cleared away and the ascent made easier.

Presently the report of cannon was heard from up the river: the batteries of Sillery and Samos were firing at the rearmost of the boats and at Holmes' squadron. Howe and his Light Infantry were detached to silence them, which they effectually did; and meanwhile the disembarkation proceeded rapidly. As fast as the boats were emptied they went back to fetch the second division from the ships and Burton's men from the opposite shore. Before the sun was well up the whole force of forty-five hundred men had accomplished the ascent, and was filing across the plain at the summit of the heights.

Wolfe went forward to reconnoitre. The ground on which he stood formed part of the high plateau which ends in the promontory of Quebec. About a mile to eastward of the landing-place was a tract of grass, known as the plains of Abraham, fairly level ground for the most part, though broken by patches of corn and clumps of bushes, and bounded on the south by the heights of the St. Lawrence and to north by those of the St. Charles. On these plains, where the plateau is less than a mile wide, Wolfe chose his position for the expected battle.

His situation, despite the skilful execution of the movement which brought his army across Montcalm's line of communication, was no secure nor enviable one, for besides Montcalm's army and the garrison of Quebec in his front, he had also to reckon with Bougainville's detachment in his rear.

His only chance of success was that the French should allow him to beat them in detail, that, in fact, they should bring out their main army and give him opportunity to crush it in front, before Bougainville should have time to operate effectively in his rear. But there was no reason why the French should do anything of the kind; and Wolfe's dispositions needed to be regulated accordingly. The extent of the ground was too great to permit order of battle in more than one line; and it was in one line that he prepared to meet the main force from the side of Quebec.

The right wing rested on the brink of the heights above the St. Lawrence, and here was stationed a single platoon of the Twenty-Eighth. Next it, in succession from right to left, stood the Thirty-Fifth, three companies of the Louisburg grenadiers, [4] the remainder of the Twenty-Eighth, the Forty-Third, Forty-Seventh, Fraser's Highlanders, and the Fifty-Eighth. Straight through the centre of the position, midway between the Forty-Seventh and Fraser's, ran the road from Sillery to Quebec, and here was posted a single light field-gun [5] which had been dragged up from Wolfe's Cove. On the extreme left, beyond the flank of the Fifty-Eighth, ran the road from Sainte Foy to Quebec, with a few scattered houses on the south side and patches of bushes and coppice beyond it.

The line, being three ranks deep, was not long enough to rest its left on this road, much less on the heights above the St. Charles, so the Fifteenth Foot was thrown back *en potence* to prevent the turning of the left flank. The second battalion of the Sixtieth and the Forty-Eighth Foot were stationed in rear, the one on the left and the other on the right, in eight subdivisions, with wide intervals. Two companies of the Fifty-Eighth were left to guard the landing-place, the third battalion of the Sixtieth was detached to the right rear to preserve communication with it; and finally Howe's Light Infantry occupied a wood far in rear, evidently to hold Bougainville in check. Monckton commanded the right and Murray the left of the fighting line, while Townsend took charge of the scattered troops which did duty for a

4. The grenadier companies of the 22nd, 40th and 45th.
5. It should seem that a second gun was brought up in the middle of the action.

reserve. Wolfe in person remained with Monckton's brigade. [6] Probably he anticipated that Montcalm would attempt to turn his right and so cut off his retreat.

Meanwhile Montcalm had passed a troubled night. The false attack of the fleet on Beauport had kept him in continual anxiety; and he was still more disquieted at daybreak to hear the sound of the cannon of Samos and Sillery above the city. He sent an officer to the Governor's quarters in Quebec for information, but received no answer; so at six o'clock he rode up to look for himself, when on reaching the right of his camp he caught sight, over the St. Charles, of an ominous band of scarlet stretched across the heights two miles away. His countenance fell. "This is a serious business," he said, and he despatched an *aide-de-camp* at full gallop to bring up the troops from the right and centre of the camp of Beauport.

The men, only lately relieved from the manning of the entrenchments, got under arms and streamed away in hot haste across the bridge of the St. Charles and through the narrow streets of the city— Indians, Canadians, and regulars all alike stirred by the sudden approach of danger. Further reconnaissance filled Montcalm with still greater dismay. It was not a mere detachment, but practically the entire British Army that had found its way to the heights between him and Montreal.

Meanwhile Vaudreuil, the Governor of Quebec, who was also commander-in-chief, was not to be found; and there was unity neither of direction nor of obedience. Montcalm applied to Ramesay, who commanded the garrison of Quebec, for twenty-five field-guns which were mounted in one of the batteries: Ramesay declared that he needed them for his own defence and would spare but three. Then there was anxious waiting for the troops from the left of Beauport's camp, which for some reason never came. All was confusion, perplexity, and distraction.

In such circumstances Montcalm appears to have succumbed to nervous strain and to have lost his wits. He held a hasty council of war with his principal officers and decided to fight at once. He was afraid, it seems, lest Wolfe should be reinforced or lest he might entrench himself. Yet there was no occasion for extreme haste. Another two hours would have sufficed, if not to bring up the missing troops from Beauport, at all events to procure more guns and to send a messenger

6. The brigades had been reconstituted on the 7th of September (see *Wolfe's Orders*), but the new order was not adhered to in the action.

by a safe route to concert measures with Bougainville; and the day was yet young.

The supplies of the French were failing, it is true, but their army was not starving; and from whence was Wolfe himself, with Bougainville in his rear, to draw his supplies even supposing that he did entrench himself? The British had two days' provisions with them, but for all further supply they must depend on a single zigzag path wide enough for but one man abreast. Even supposing that Montcalm could not succeed in obtaining the thirty field-guns for which he asked, and which if obtained would almost inevitably have blasted the British army off the field, there was nothing to prevent him from manoeuvring with a superior force to keep the British under arms until nightfall, while his Indians and irregulars, of whom he had abundance, harried the British right flank in front and rear under shelter of the scrub, and hindered the bringing up of further stores.

What would have been the condition of Wolfe's army on the following morning after a second night under arms, and what opening might there not have been for successful attack? But it was not to be. Whether Montcalm was spurred on by the impatience of his own half -distracted force, or whether he simply gave way to nervous exhaustion, must remain uncertain. At any rate he resolved with the five thousand troops that were with him to accept battle at once.

By nine o'clock his line of battle was formed, some six hundred yards from the British position. On his right, resting on the road to Sainte Foy was a battalion of Canadian militia, and next to it in succession the regular regiments of Bèarn and La Sarre. Next to these, in column on either side of the road to Sillery, were the regiments of Guienne and Languedoc, and to their left regiment Roussillon and another battalion of militia. On the extreme right and left some two thousand Indians and Canadians swarmed forward in skirmishing order in advance of the line of battle. It was with the fire of these sharpshooters that the action began. There was good cover for them not only on the flanks but also among the scattered bushes in the front.

Wolfe threw out skirmishers to meet them, and the fusillade became lively, especially on the British left, where Townsend's men began to fall fast. So severe became this pressure on the left that Townsend, alarmed for his flank, brought up the second battalion of the Sixtieth to the left of the Fifty-Eighth, detailed part of them to drive the Canadians from the houses by the road and doubled the remainder back *en potence* in line with the Fifteenth; while at the same time the Light

Infantry was called up in support of the Fifteenth to strengthen the flank still further.

Thus before the action was well begun the rear-guard and half of the reserve was practically absorbed in the fighting line. On the British right, where the French sharpshooters could not get round the flank, their fire was by no means so deadly; but it does not appear that either of these attacks formed part of any settled plan of Montcalm, for by throwing the mass of his skirmishers against the British left he might have made them very formidable.

Meanwhile Montcalm's three field-guns had opened fire, and were answered by the single gun on the Sillery road with great effect. So the minutes dragged on, until at a little before ten the French line advanced with loud shouts to the true attack, the regulars in the centre moving steadily, a long streak of white edged on either hand with red and with blue, and the militia striving to move as steadily on the flanks. The English, who until now had been lying down, then sprang to their feet and stood steady with recovered arms. At a range of two hundred yards the French muskets opened fire but with little effect, while much confusion and delay was caused by the Canadian militia who, true to their instincts as skirmishers, threw themselves flat on the ground to reload.

Wolfe was shot through the wrist, but he merely wrapped his handkerchief round the wound, and called to the men to be steady and reserve their fire. The French recovered their order somewhat and again came on, filling the air with their cries, while the British stood calm, silent and immovable, knowing their chief and trusting him. [7] Nearer and nearer drew the parti-coloured line, gayer and gayer as the blue and scarlet facings on the white coats came into view, brighter and brighter as the detail of metal buttons and accoutrements cleared themselves from the distance, till at length the time was come.

Thirty-five yards only separated the opposing arrays, when the word rang out, the still red line sprang into life, the recovered muskets leaped forward into a long bristling bar, and with one deafening crash, the most perfect volley ever fired on battlefield burst forth as if from a single monstrous weapon, from end to end of the British line. A dense bank of smoke blotted the French from sight, and from behind it there rose a horrible din of clattering arms, and savage oaths and agonised cries. The sharp clink of ramrods broke in upon the sound as the Brit-

---

7. "There is no necessity for firing very fast: a cool well-levelled fire is much more destructive and formidable than the quickest fire in confusion." *Wolfe's Orders.*

ish reloaded; and when the smoke rolled away, the gay line was seen to be shivered to fragments, while the bright coats strewed the ground like swathes of gaudy flowers. There was hardly a bullet of that volley that had not struck home.

Montcalm, himself unhurt and conspicuous on a black charger, galloped frantically up and down his shattered ranks in a vain effort to restore order. Wolfe gave the order to advance, and after one more volley the scarlet line strode forward with bayonet and claymore to complete the rout. There was nothing to stop the British, nothing even to gall them except the fire of a few sharpshooters hidden in the scrub. Wolfe himself led them at the head of the Twenty-Eighth. A bullet struck him in the groin, but he paused not a moment and was still striding on, when another ball passed through his lungs. He staggered forward, still vainly striving to keep on his feet. "Support me, support me," he gasped to an officer who was close to him, "lest my gallant fellows should see me fall."

Two or three men fell out and carried him to the rear, but his fall was noticed by few; and the victorious line pressed on. Some of the sharpshooters continued to fire from behind the shrubs and required to be driven out. Others taking cover nearer to the town opened a biting fire on the Highlanders who, charging as usual with the claymore only, suffered much loss in the attempt to force so wily an enemy from the bush. But other regiments came up and did the work for them with the musket, and thenceforward no further stand was made by the French, but Montcalm's whole force broke up and fled in wild confusion towards the town. He himself, borne away in the rush of the fugitives, was shot through the body, but being supported in the saddle rode in through the gates. "It is nothing, nothing," he called to the shrieking women who saw the red stains on his white uniform; "don't distress yourselves over me, good people."

He was lifted from his horse and borne into a surgeon's house to die. The panic among the French increased. Their chief was dying, his second mortally wounded; and among the terrified mob that fled by the St. Charles there rose a cry to destroy the bridge of boats, lest the English should break into the camp of Beauport. This insane movement, which would have sacrificed the whole of the fugitives who had not yet crossed the river, was checked by one or two officers who still kept their wits about them; but none the less the French were not only beaten but demoralised, and the victory of the British was complete.

But the victors also had lost the services both of their general and his second. Monckton had been severely wounded by a musket-shot which for the present disabled him from duty, and Wolfe had been carried to the rear more dead than alive. He begged his bearers to set him down, and refused to see a surgeon. "There is no need," he said, "it is all over with me"; and he sank into unconsciousness.

"How they run," cried out one of the attendants, as he watched the French flying before the red-coats.

"Who run?" asked Wolfe, waking suddenly to life.

"The enemy, Sir, they give way everywhere,"

"Go one of you to Colonel Burton," ordered the dying general with great earnestness, "and tell him to march Webb's regiment [8]down to Charles River to cut off the retreat from the bridge." He ceased, and turned on his side. "Now, God be praised, I will die in peace," he murmured; and so died.

With his death and the disabling of Monckton the command devolved upon Townsend, who had no sooner assumed it than he found the rear of the army threatened by Bougainville. Turning upon this new enemy with two battalions and two field-guns he soon forced him to retire; and then, the pursuit being ended, he proceeded to entrench himself on the battlefield. The losses of the British were trifling compared with the magnitude of the success, amounting to no more than six hundred and thirty of all ranks killed and wounded. [9] The chief sufferers were the Highlanders, during their onslaught with the claymore, and the Fifteenth, Fifty-Eighth and second battalion of the Sixtieth, who bore the brunt of the sharpshooting on the left flank.

Before midnight the entrenchments had made good progress, and cannon had been brought up to defend them. A battery also had been mounted at the northern angle of the town, and the French hospital, full of sick and wounded men, had been taken. Nothing is said of the exhaustion of the troops, who had been on duty continuously for at least thirty hours.

Meanwhile utter confusion reigned in the French camp. Vaudreuil called a council of war, and there was tumultuous debate. A messenger was sent to the dying Montcalm for advice, and returned with the reply that there were three courses open, to retreat up the river, to fight again, or to surrender the colony. There was much to be said for fighting, for with Bougainville's force the French could still bring superior

8. The 28th.

9. Killed—10 officers, 48 men; wounded—37 officers, 535 men.

numbers into the field; still more to be said for the defence of Quebec; but the demoralisation was too deep to permit any bold action.

At nine o'clock in the evening Vaudreuil gave the order to retreat, and, the word once uttered, the entire French force streamed away in disorderly and disgraceful flight to the post of Jacques Carrier, thirty miles up the St. Lawrence. The only instructions left with the garrison of Quebec were to surrender as soon as provisions should fail. Well was it for Montcalm, always a brave and faithful soldier, that his deliverance came to him before the dawn of another day.

Townsend for his part pushed his trenches forward against Quebec with the greatest energy. The French, despite their precipitate retreat, were still in superior force in his rear; and though certainly demoralised might rally on joining the unbeaten troops of Lévis, and imbibe new courage under the leadership of that excellent officer. It was therefore imperative to press the garrison hard while still overpowered by the despairing sense of its isolation. On the 17th of September the British ships of war moved up against the Lower Town, and a scarlet column approached the walls from the meadows of the St. Charles.

The French drums beat to arms, but the Canadian militia refused to turn out, and the white flag was hoisted. An officer was sent to Townsend's quarters to gain time, if possible, by prolonging negotiations. Townsend's answer was peremptory: unless the town were surrendered by eleven o'clock, he would take it by storm; and on this Ramesay signed the capitulation. It was none too soon. Before the messenger with the signed articles had reached Townsend, Canadian horsemen arrived with provisions and with a cheering message that help was at hand; and on the very next morning Lévis marched out from Jacques Cartier, only to learn that he was just too late.

On the afternoon of the 18th the British entered the city, and during the following weeks were employed in strengthening the defences and making provision against the winter; for it had been decided that the fortress must be held at all risks. Monckton was still too far disabled to assume command; Townsend, fresh from the House of Commons, had no mind for such dreary duty as winter-quarters; so Brigadier Murray was left as governor with a garrison of seven thousand five hundred men, his battalions being strengthened by drafts from the Sixty-Second and Sixty-Ninth, which were serving on board the fleet. At the end of October Admiral Saunders fired his farewell salute and dropped down the river with his fleet, carrying with him the embalmed remains of Wolfe, to be laid by his father's body in the parish church of Greenwich.

So ended the first stage of the conquest of Canada, with better fortune than might have been expected; for there is no gainsaying the fact that the concert of operations intended by Pitt and designed by Amherst had broken down. It should seem indeed that the scheme was too complex, that too much was attempted with the resources at command, that the combination of the various enterprises was too intricate to admit of complete success in a wild and distant country, where the campaigning season was so strictly bounded by the climate. Amherst's operations depended greatly on the help given to him by the Provincials, and the colonial assemblies whatever their good-will were always dilatory, while sometimes, as in the case of Pennsylvania, they were intolerably recalcitrant.

Again, though drafts had been sent to the general to make good the losses of the previous campaign, [10] these were not nearly sufficient to fill the gaps made by the slaughter of Ticonderoga and the bitter cold of a Canadian winter. Significantly enough, also, no care had been taken to provide the garrison of Louisburg, most arctic of quarters, even with coverlets, so that the casualties in the winter were far greater than they should have been. [11] Again, it had been ordained that Hopson should reinforce Amherst when his work at Martinique was done, but this arrangement also had broken down; and the least forethought as to the waste of a tropical campaign would have shown that it should not have been reckoned on. The result was that Amherst and Wolfe found themselves with insufficient troops, and that as a natural consequence the former was obliged to cut the margin of his several operations too fine.

The death of Prideaux, an excellent officer, was a great misfortune, though Johnson finished his work at Niagara efficiently enough. Stanwix also, after overcoming vast difficulties of transport, succeeded in penetrating to Pittsburg; but here the operations of both columns came to an end. The Ohio happened to be so low that Stanwix could not send up a battalion, as he had been bidden, to reinforce Gage for his advance to La Galette; and Gage, who was not a very enterprising man, to Amherst's great disappointment thought himself not strong enough to move in consequence. On Amherst's own failure to reach Montreal comment has already been passed; but it should be remembered that the whole burden of the preparations for Wolfe's expedi-

10. *Secretary's Common Letter Book,* 8th September 1759. 2150 drafts were sent.
11. Whitmore (Louisburg) to Pitt, 22nd January 1759.

tion was laid upon him, and that Wolfe gratefully acknowledged the thoroughness of the work. Still the fact remains that the diversions from south and west were an almost total failure, and that Wolfe was consequently obliged to perform his difficult task unaided.

Fortune was against the British in that the weather delayed the assembling of Wolfe's army at Louisburg; for those few lost weeks might easily have made the entire difference to the campaign. Wolfe, with an inadequate force, was driven to his wits' end to solve the problem assigned to him; and it is quite incontestable that the credit for the fall of Quebec belongs rather to the Navy than to the Army. The names of Saunders and of Holmes are little remembered; and the fame of James Cook the master, whose skill and diligence did much to reveal the unknown channel of the St. Lawrence, is swallowed up in that of Captain James Cook the navigator.

Still the fact remains unaltered. It was the audacity of Holmes and his squadron in running the gauntlet of the batteries of Quebec which first threatened the supplies and communications of the city, and forced Montcalm to weaken his main army by detaching Bougainville. It was the terrible restless energy of the same squadron, ever moving up and down the river, which wore out the limbs of the French soldiers and the nerves of their officers; and to the Navy fully as much as to the Army is due the praise for the movement that finally set Wolfe and his battalions on the heights of Abraham. But in truth this last most delicate and critical operation was so admirably thought out and executed by the officers of both services that it must abide for ever a masterpiece in its kind. The British navy and army working, as at Quebec, in concord and harmony under loyal and able chiefs, are indeed not easily baffled.

It still remains for enquiry why Wolfe did not take earlier advantage of the opportunities opened to him by the fleet; and even after allowance has been made for his constant illness, the answer is not readily found. The measures which led to the decisive action were, as has been told, taken on the advice of his brigadiers, and, if Montcalm had not succumbed to positive infatuation, would very likely have brought Wolfe to a court-martial. But if instead of wasting the whole of August in futile efforts below Quebec, Wolfe had shifted his operations forthwith to the west of the city, it seems at least probable that he could have attained his object without hazarding that desperate cast on the plains of Abraham.

It would presumably have been open to him to gain the heights as he gained them ultimately, to have overwhelmed Bougainville's posts piecemeal, as was done as far as Sillery by a small detachment on the morning of the battle, and to have entrenched himself in the most suitable of them. Then having cut the French communications by land and water, he could have forced Montcalm either to abandon Quebec or to fight on his own terms. But it is easy to be wise after the event; and a brilliant success, however fortunate, is rightly held to cover all errors. Moreover, the praise for the perfection of drill and discipline which won the victory with a single volley is all Wolfe's own. Still it seems to be a fair criticism that the general was slow to perceive the real weakness of Montcalm's position and the vital spot laid open to him by the fleet for a deadly thrust. The consequence was that the work was but half done and, as shall now be seen, only narrowly escaped undoing.

CHAPTER 16

Blood in the Snow: Sainte Foy

The city of Quebec when the British entered into possession was little better than a shapeless mass of ruins, having been reduced to that state by the guns of the fleet. The population was thoroughly demoralised, and given over to theft and pillage; liquor was abundant and the British soldier was thirsty; in fact it needed all Murray's firmness to restore any kind of order.[1] In December severe weather began in earnest, and the effects of bad quarters, bad food, insufficient clothing and insufficient fuel speedily made themselves felt. The sentries were relieved every hour, yet it was impossible to keep them free of frost-bite. The Highlanders despite their natural hardihood suffered more than their comrades, the kilt being but a sorry protection against a Canadian winter; and they were only relieved by a supply of long woollen hose knitted for them, perhaps as much for decency's as for charity's sake, by the nuns of the city.

Still the men remained cheerful, for they were kept constantly at work cutting fuel and dragging it in sledges to their quarters, an errand on which they set forth always with muskets as well as with axes, from fear of Indians and bushrangers. Nevertheless their sufferings were great. Fifty men were frost-bitten on a single day while employed on this duty; three days later sixty-five more were similarly afflicted, and before Christmas there were over a hundred and fifty cases.[2] This, however, would have been a small matter but for the more deadly scourge that was added to it. The garrison was victualled

---

1. Murray's *Journal*, 14th Nov. 1759. "So much drunkenness that I recalled all licences, and ordered every man found drunk to receive twenty lashes every morning until he acknowledged where he got the drink, and to forfeit his allowance of rum for six weeks."
2. Murray's *Journal*, 14th, 17th, 24th December 1759.

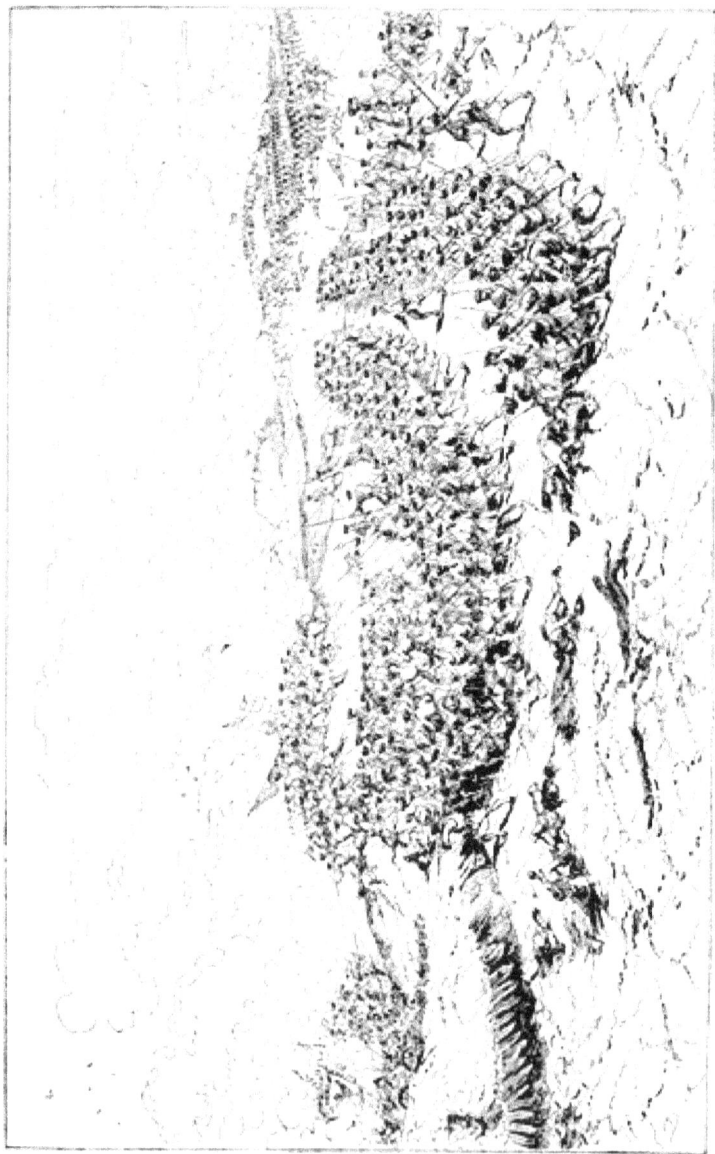

THE BATTLE OF SAINTE FOY

entirely with salt provisions; it was impossible to procure fresh meat for the men; and scurvy grew and increased until there was hardly a soldier in the ranks, even among those reckoned fit for duty, who was wholly free from the disease.

With such a plague in his midst Murray might well feel apprehensive for the safety of Quebec against the enemy without the walls, for ever since the British occupation of the city the French had made no secret of their intention to recapture it. Murray had established two fortified posts a few miles to westward of Quebec at Sainte Foy and Old Lorette; while the French had established themselves at St. Augustine, only two days' march from the gates, from which position it was soon necessary to expel them. Petty skirmishes such as this were frequent, but ended always with so easy advantage to the British that the troops began to think themselves invincible. Repeated intelligence, however, still arrived of French designs against Quebec, vague enough at first, but, as the winter wore on, gradually assuming more definite form. Lévis, the ablest officer left to the French since the fall of Montcalm, was in fact straining every nerve to organise and equip a force of overwhelming strength for the purpose. He had full information of the state of Murray's army and knew that he had but to bide his time for scurvy to do the best part of his work for him. At the end of March he heard that half of the British were on the sick-list, and the report was not far from the truth. By the middle of April Murray had barely three thousand men fit for duty, while no fewer than seven hundred were lying in the snowdrifts, waiting till spring should unbind the frozen ground to give them a grave.

On the 17th of April Murray, learning that the preparations of the French were complete, occupied the mouth of Cap Rouge River to prevent a landing at that point. Four days later Lévis set out with about seven thousand men, half of them regular troops, and a fleet of *bateaux* escorted by two frigates and by several smaller craft. The river was not yet free from ice, the weather was bad, and navigation was difficult; but on the 26th the army, reinforced by the garrisons of several outlying stations to nearly nine thousand men, landed at St. Augustine and marched upon the British advanced posts. The British at once fell back from Cap Rouge and Old Lorette upon Sainte Foy. Lévis followed after them all night, despite the difficulties of half-thawed ice and driving rain and tempest, and at daybreak arrived before Sainte Foy to find every house occupied by the British and their cannon playing on his columns as they emerged from the forest.

Murray, warned by the information of a French gunner, who had been picked up half dead from the floating ice in the St. Lawrence, had marched out with half of the garrison to cover the retreat of his advanced parties. The position which he occupied was strong, and Lévis being ignorant of the weakness of his numbers would not venture to attack, but resolved to wait until nightfall and then move round the British left flank. Murray therefore was able to retire in safety to Quebec, while Lévis occupied Sainte Foy and pushed his light troops forward to Sillery.

Murray's position now was none of the pleasantest. The fortifications of Quebec were in no condition to withstand an energetic cannonade, and the ground was still frozen so hard that it was impossible for him to throw up entrenchments, as he had long desired, outside the walls. The only alternative open to him was to sally out and fight Lévis, at odds of one against two, and beat him if he could. Murray was young, daring and fired by the example of Wolfe; his army was, as he said, in the habit of beating the enemy; [3] and he had a fine train of artillery. He therefore resolved to go out and fight. Accordingly at half-past six on the morning of the 28th he marched out of Quebec at the head of all the troops that he could muster, a bare three thousand men, with three howitzers and twenty field-pieces, and drew them up on the ground which Montcalm had occupied on the famous 13th of September.

The force was formed in one line of two brigades, the right or Burton's brigade consisting, from right to left, of the Fifteenth, Fifty-Eighth, second battalion of the Sixtieth, and Forty-Eighth regiments; the left or Fraser's brigade of the Forty-Third, Forty-Seventh, Fraser's Highlanders, and the Twenty-Eighth. The Thirty-Fifth and third battalion of the Sixtieth were posted in reserve in rear of the centre, while the Light Infantry and the Provincial rangers stood wide on the right and left flanks. The field-guns were distributed in pairs to each battalion.

Moving forward to reconnoitre, Murray perceived that the French line was not yet formed. That Lévis had chosen his ground was clear, for he had occupied two block-houses built by the British above Anse du Foulon at the southern edge of the plateau, as well as a house and a fortified windmill at the northern brink, and had extended his vanguard along the ridge between these two points. But the main body was still debouching in columns from Sillery Wood, a mile or more in

3. Murray to Pitt, 25th May 1759.

rear, and two brigades only were as yet deployed by the block-house to form the French right wing.

Thinking the opportunity favourable, Murray ordered an immediate advance; and his whole line moved forward, the men dragging their guns with them in the intervals between battalions. The ground was for the most part still covered with snow, which in some places was piled up in drifts and everywhere soft and sodden with rain; and the tramp of three thousand men soon turned the soil into a sea of mud. Arrived at the ground where Wolfe's army had stood, the line halted, and the guns unlimbering opened so destructive a fire on the French columns that Lévis ordered the battalions of his left to fall back to the woods. The manoeuvre was not executed without confusion, and Murray, elated by his apparent success, ordered the line to renew its advance, inclining to its right.

This movement, however, brought Burton's brigade on to low ground, where the melting snow was knee-deep and the guns could not be worked with effect. The British Light Infantry attacked the windmill and houses on the French left with great spirit, carried them in spite of a desperate resistance, and pressed on in pursuit of the retreating French. But now the battalions of the French left, no longer checked by the fire of artillery, dashed out of the woods in skirmishing order and falling on the rash pursuers fairly overwhelmed them. Over two hundred of the Light Infantry were killed and wounded, and the few survivors hurrying back in confusion upon Burton's brigade prevented it from firing on the advancing enemy. The French seized the opportunity to reform their broken ranks and the combat was hotly maintained for more than an hour, until ammunition for the British artillery failed, the tumbrils being immovably fixed in the snowdrifts.

On Murray's left his hasty advance was little less disastrous. The block-houses were indeed carried and held for a time, but the French fell back into the woods only to advance again in overwhelming force when the fire of the British artillery failed, and to extend themselves along the British front and flank. The two battalions of the reserve were called up and the fight was maintained with indomitable stubbornness; but with both flanks turned the efforts of the British were hopeless, and Murray gave the word to fall back.

The men, though but two in three of them remained unhurt, were furious at the order. "Damn it, what is falling back but retreating!" they said; but there was no help for it. So first the left brigade and then the right retired, cursing as they went. Some of the regiments tried to carry off their guns with them, but finding this impossible owing to deep snow and mud spiked and abandoned them. The French followed in pursuit, hoping to cut them off from the city; but Lévis perceiving the orderliness of the retreat judged it more prudent to recall his troops, and Murray brought back the remnant of his force in safety to Quebec.

So ended the action of Sainte Foy after two hours of stern and bloody work. The loss of the British amounted to a thousand killed and wounded or a full third of the entire force. The Fifteenth, Twenty-Eighth, and Highlanders [4] were, after the Light Infantry, the greatest sufferers, but in the attenuated state of the battalions it is probable that in seven out of the ten there fell at least one man in three. The loss of the French was admitted to have exceeded eight hundred. Altogether it was an unfortunate affair, though it cannot be called discreditable to the troops. Murray was misled by overweening confidence in his men and miscalculation of the spirit of the French. His past experience doubtless partly excused the mistake; but even if he had failed to grasp that Lévis was a man who could restore confidence to demoralised troops, he might at least have guessed that he would bring up fresh regiments, who had not learned to fear the red-coats, to meet him.

As things were, he sacrificed the advantages of his position and of his superiority in artillery and found himself shut up within the miserable fortifications of Quebec, with his force reduced to twenty-four hundred men, nominally fit for duty, but in reality, to use the expressive words of one of them, "half-starved scorbutic skeletons."

Murray, however, rose to the emergency with a spirit worthy of a British officer. The troops were at first inclined to break loose from discipline, but Murray hanged the chief offender, staved in all the rum-barrels of the sutlers and quickly restored order. Then every soul of the garrison fell to work to strengthen the defences. Officers yoked themselves to cannon and plied pickaxe and spade, and the men with such an example before them strained themselves to the utmost.

In a short time one hundred and fifty guns were mounted and at work on the walls of Quebec, while the French, however they might toil at their trenches in the stubborn soil of the plateau, had hardly

---

4. A wounded Highland officer who had fought under Lord George Murray at Culloden was heard to ejaculate, "From April battles and Murray generals, Good Lord deliver us." Murray, who lacked neither humour nor generosity, came to see him next morning and wished him better deliverance and a different prayer in his next action.

brought up a single cannon to answer them. None the less incessant labour and bad food were telling heavily on the enfeebled strength of the garrison, when on the 9th of May the *Lowestoft* frigate sailed up to Quebec with the news that a squadron was at the mouth of the river and would arrive within a few days. The tidings put new heart into the besieged, though had Lévis ventured on an assault they would have found it hard to repel him.

On the 15th two more British men-of-war arrived at Quebec, and next morning two frigates sailed up above the city, attacked and destroyed Lévis' ships and with them the French supplies of food and ammunition. That same evening Lévis raised the siege and retreated with precipitation, leaving behind him forty guns, the whole of his material for the siege, and every man of his sick and wounded. Murray marched at dawn to fall upon his rear, but though he captured many stragglers failed to overtake the main body. Thus Quebec was saved; and the advent of spring, together with a supply of fresh provisions, soon turned Murray's sickly battalions into an army fit for service in the field.

PLAN of the BATTLE of STe FOY

Reference

British French
Redoubts Blockhouses
Roads Woods

SCALE OF FEET
1000   0   1000   2000

A - First position of the British
B -   "   "   "
C - Entrenchments made by
    Lévis after the battle
A' -
B' - French

Cape Diamond

St. John's B.
St. Ursula B.
St. Louis Bastion
Diamond B.
St. John's Gate
St. Louis Gate
La Roche

Ste Foy Road
Road La Sillery

R. CABEAU

BUTTRIE'S BOT

HEIGHTS OF

ABRAHAM

Mill

Schapman's

FOREST OF SILLERY

Foulon

CHAPTER 18

Near Path's End

During these miserable months of cold, privation, and disease Amherst had been maturing his plans for a decisive campaign. Pitt had enjoined the capture of Montreal upon him as the principal object, and had resolved to demolish the useless fortress of Louisburg, thereby releasing the garrison for active service. [1] The provincial assemblies were called upon once more to furnish large contingents of troops for a supreme effort, and the final blow was about to fall. Amherst's design was to invade Canada simultaneously from east, west, and south. Murray was to ascend the St. Lawrence from Quebec; Brigadier Haviland was to break in by Lake Champlain; and Amherst himself was to lead the main army down the St. Lawrence from Lake Ontario.

Of the three lines of advance Amherst's was not only the longest but the most difficult and dangerous, owing to the rapids which obstruct the navigation of the St. Lawrence; but on the other hand the movement would cut off the retreat of the French army to westward and force it back upon Montreal, where Haviland and Murray would close in upon it and fairly throttle it. The plan was delicate in the extreme and called for the greatest nicety of calculation, for the three armies must start from three different points hundreds of miles apart without possibility of inter-communication, and yet arrive at their goal together, lest the French should concentrate and overwhelm Murray's or Haviland's corps in detail. The principal French posts for barring the lines of advance were Ile aux Noix at the head of Lake Ontario, Sorel on the eastern side of Montreal, and La Galette at the head of the rapids of the St. Lawrence.

The year opened ill for Amherst. In March he was compelled to

---

1. Pitt to Amherst, 7th January, 9th February 1760.

send thirteen hundred men [2] to the south to quell a rising of Chero-kee Indians; and he had not long communicated his instructions to Murray when he received tidings of the defeat of Sainte Foy. He at once summoned two battalions from Louisburg to reinforce Murray, but it was not until late in June that he was relieved by news of the safety of Quebec. The provincial governments also were as usual a sore trial and the cause of much vexatious delay; [3] but Amherst was a man of tenacity and patience who never lost sight of his object nor relaxed his industry for a moment. At length, when midsummer was fully past, the net which he had woven began to close round the French.

Murray was the first to move. His garrison had rapidly recovered health and strength, and by July he was able to pick out twenty-two hundred men for the advance on Montreal, while still leaving sev-enteen hundred behind him for the garrison of Quebec. On the 14th of July his little column embarked in thirty-two vessels with a number of boats and *bateaux*, and on the following day set sail up the St. Lawrence, leaving Lord Rollo to follow with the Twenty-Second and Fortieth Regiments, which had arrived from Louisburg. Murray advanced slowly, skirmishing with small parties of the enemy which hovered about the flotilla on the shore, and disarming the inhabitants as he passed.

On the 4th of August he reached Three Rivers, where lay a de-tachment of the French Army; but without delaying to attack it, he passed on to Sorel, where Bourlamaque and M. Dumas with some four thousand men were entrenched along both banks of the river. These officers had been instructed to follow up the flotilla as it moved, so British and French alike advanced towards Montreal, where Lévis lay with the main French Army. Murray, meanwhile, by rigour to-wards the recalcitrant and lenity towards the submissive, persuaded half of Bourlamaque's militia to yield up its arms and take an oath of neutrality. By the 24th, being within nine leagues of Montreal, he sent out a party to seek news of Haviland, and then moving up to Ile Sainte Thérése, just below Montreal, he encamped and awaited the coming of his colleagues.

Haviland, meanwhile, had embarked in the third week of August at Crown Point, with two battalions of regulars, and with Provincials and Indians sufficient to raise his force to thirty-four hundred men. Four days brought him to Bougainville's position at Ile aux Noix, where

2. 1st Royals and Montgomery's Highlanders. Amherst to Pitt, 8th March 1760.
3. Amherst to Pitt, 21st June 1760.

he landed, erected batteries, and opened fire on the fort; while at the same time a party of rangers dragged three guns to the rear of the position and turned them upon Bougainville's sloops of war, which got under way in all haste and stranded in the next bend of the river. Thus Bougainville's communications with the next post, St. John's, down the River Richelieu, were severed, and, as Amherst had foreseen, [4] he was compelled to abandon the island. He joined M. Roquemaure at St. John's with infinite difficulty by a night march through the forest; and both officers falling back from St. John's and Chambly waited with Bourlamaque on the banks of the St. Lawrence, where their force melted away fast through desertion. Haviland opened communications with Murray, and both awaited the approach of Amherst.

The main army had assembled at Oswego during July, Amherst himself arriving on the 9th, but it was not until the first week of August that the last of the appointed regiments appeared at the rendezvous. The force consisted of eight weak battalions of British, numbering less than six thousand men, with four thousand five hundred Provincials and seven hundred Indians, or about eleven thousand in all. The flotilla for the transport of the army was made up of nearly eight hundred whale-boats and *bateaux*, and was escorted by gunboats. On the 10th of August the entire force was embarked and by the 15th it had reached Oswegatchie or La Galette, on the site of the present Ogdensburg. Here a French brig of ten guns was attacked and captured by the gun-boats, and the flotilla pursued its way among the Thousand Islands.

On an islet at the head of the rapids stood a French post named Fort Lévis, with a garrison of three hundred men, which Amherst forthwith invested, and after three days' cannonade reduced to surrender. Repair of the fort and of his boats detained him until the 30th, and on the 31st the expedition entered upon the most critical of its work, the descent of the rapids.

On the 1st of September the flotilla was compelled to proceed in single file, but all went well until the 4th, when the most dangerous of the rapids was reached. On that day over sixty boats were wrecked or damaged and eighty-four men were drowned: but the passage was accomplished without molestation from the enemy, though large numbers of Canadians were on the watch on the banks.

The next day was consumed in repairs, and on the 6th, the last rapid having been passed, the boats glided down to La Chine, nine miles

8. Amherst to Haviland, 12th June 1760.

from Montreal, on the left bank of the St. Lawrence. Here the army landed unopposed, marched straight upon Montreal and encamped beneath the walls on the eastern side: while Haviland on the 8th arrived on the southern shore against Amherst's camp. Amherst was a little late, having been delayed by the resistance of Fort Lévis. Had he been content to ignore it and simply to cut it off from Montreal, he, Murray and Haviland would have met, punctual to a day, on the 29th of August. As it was the junction was sufficiently complete, and the work of the campaign was practically done.

Bougainville, Bourlamaque, and Roquemaure had crossed over to Montreal with the few regular troops remaining with them, for the whole of their militia had melted away, and even the regulars had been greatly reduced by desertion. Thus the army assembled at Montreal, the sole force that remained for the defence of Canada, amounted to barely twenty-five hundred men, demoralised in order, in spirit, and in discipline. Around the city lay an hostile army of seventeen thousand men; the fortifications were contemptible except for defence against Indians, and Amherst's cannon were already moving up from La Chine. The French governor called a council of war, which resolved that resistance was hopeless.

Articles of capitulation were accordingly drawn up, and carried on the 7th by Bougainville to Amherst. The condition on which the French laid greatest stress was that they should march out with the honours of war; but this Amherst flatly refused. The troops, he said, must lay down their arms and serve no further during the present war: the French had played so inhuman a part in stirring up the Indians to treachery and barbarity of every kind, that he was determined to make an example of them. It is probable that the general referred only to the massacre of the wounded after the defeats at Fort William Henry, Ticonderoga, and the Monongahela; but the reckoning to be paid went back to earlier times. There were the wrongs, the encroachment and the double-dealing of a full century to be redressed; and the time for payment was come.

In vain the French pleaded for easier terms: Amherst, a man not easily turned from his purpose, remained inflexible. Accordingly on the 8th of September, despite expostulation which rose almost to the point of mutiny on the part of Lévis, the capitulation was signed, and half a continent passed into the hands of Great Britain.

CHAPTER 19

Against the Cherokees

Meanwhile, as if to crown the whole work and to redeem all past failings and misfortunes, the expedition against the Cherokee Indians had been brilliantly successful. Trifling though the affair may seem in comparison with Amherst's momentous operations in the north, it marked the banishment of the panic fear of Indians which had followed on the defeat of Braddock. The command was entrusted to Colonel Montgomery, and the force committed to him was four hundred of the First Royals, seven hundred of his own Highlanders, and a strong body of Provincials. Starting from Charlestown, Carolina, Montgomery marched up one hundred and fifty miles to the township of Ninety-Six, so called because it was supposed to be ninety-six miles from the township of Keowee, and pushed forward thence for four days through dense forest and mountainous country without finding any sign of Indians.

Concluding therefore that the Cherokees were unaware of his advance, he left all tents and baggage behind and made a forced march to surprise the savages before they could escape. The main body of the Indians, however, retired before he could reach them; and he could accomplish no more than the destruction of crops and villages, after which he returned to a fort on the frontier, having traversed no less than sixty miles over a most difficult country without a halt.

It was then resolved to begin the work anew and to make a fresh advance into the forest. On this occasion the Indians lay in wait for the British in a wooded valley and burst upon them suddenly, as they had upon Braddock, with hideous whooping and howling, and a scattered but deadly fire of rifles. The grenadiers and Light Infantry at once plunged into the forest to engage them, while the Highlanders hastened round their rear to cut off their retreat; and after a sharp action

151

of an hour the Indians were put to flight with great slaughter. This engagement cost the British over eighty men killed and wounded, twice as many as Amherst had lost by lead and steel during the whole of his advance from Oswego to Montreal. But the mere comparison of casualties is of small moment. The really weighty matter is that British officers had learned to face the difficulties which had been fatal to Braddock, and to overcome them with a light heart.

It now remained for Amherst to enforce the capitulation on the French posts of the west. The occupation of Detroit, Miamis, and Michillimackinac was entrusted to Rogers, the partisan, with his rangers, who in the course of the winter hauled down the ensign of the Bourbons and hoisted the British flag in its place. There was still to be trouble with these remote stations, but it was not to come immediately, nor directly from the French. The rest of the general's work was principally administrative. Generous terms were granted to the inhabitants, and every precaution was taken to protect them against the Indian allies of the British.

CHAPTER 20

Victory

Amherst issued a general order appealing to his troops not to disgrace their victory by any unsoldierlike behaviour or appearance of inhumanity; and the army responded to the appeal with a heartiness which amazed the Canadians. A month after the capitulation the general could report that British soldiers and Canadian peasants were joining their provisions and messing together, and that when he had ordered soldiers to leave their scattered quarters so as to be closer to their companies, the people had begged that they might not be moved. [1] Such was not the fashion in which the French were wont to treat a captured territory.

Here then for the present we may take leave of Amherst. Pitt had further tasks for him, which were to be executed as usual quietly and thoroughly. The fame of the man is lost in that of Wolfe, and yet it was he, not Wolfe, that was the conqueror of Canada. The criticism usually passed upon him is that he was sure but slow, and to some extent it is justified by facts. Yet it should be remembered that, when he took over the command, affairs in North America were in extreme confusion and disorder, and that the work assigned to him was, on a far larger and more formidable scale, that which had fallen to Cumberland in 1745. Braddock had started everything in the wrong direction. Not only had he quarrelled with the Provincials and failed to instruct his troops aright, but he had deliberately forced them to follow wrong methods.

Loudoun, again, had not improved relations with the provincial assemblies either by his correspondence with them or by his military operations. Finally Abercromby's imbecility at Ticonderoga had sacri-

---

1. Amherst to Pitt, 18th Oct. 1760.

ficed hundreds of valuable lives, disgusted the colonists, and heightened the reputation gained by the French at the Monongahela. Then Amherst took the whole of the confused business in hand, and from that moment all went smoothly and well; so smoothly indeed that people quite forgot that it had ever gone otherwise. Yet his difficulties with the Provincials were not less than those of his predecessors nor less trying to his patience than to theirs; nay, even the good-will of the colonists was sometimes as embarrassing to him as their obstruction. It must not be forgotten, moreover, that the atmosphere of young communities, such as were then the North American colonies, is most noxious to discipline.

Thus when Amherst returned from the conquest of Louisburg to Boston, not all his efforts could prevent the inhabitants of that godly city from filling his men with rum; and the same spirit of indiscipline doubtless haunted the army through all the long and dreary months of winter-quarters. There was, again, the additional complication that in the matter of forest-fighting the British had much to learn from the Provincials; and it fell to Amherst to teach his troops greater freedom and independence in action without simultaneous relaxation of discipline. He overcame all these obstacles, however, in his quiet, methodical way. Discipline never failed; for Amherst, though no martinet, could be inexorably severe. Special corps of light troops and of marksmen were organised, and the drill of the whole army was modified to suit new conditions.

It was in fact Amherst who showed the way to the reform afterwards carried out by Sir John Moore at Shorncliffe, of reducing the depth of the ranks to two men only. Such a formation would have diminished Wolfe's difficulties and materially have strengthened his dispositions on the plains of Abraham: but apparently so important an innovation never occurred to him. Amherst never fought a great action, so his improvements were never put to the test; but this does not impair his credit as a soldier of forethought and originality.

But the most remarkable quality in Amherst was his talent for organisation. The difficulties of transport in the Canada of his day were appalling. The American historian Parkman says:

> Canada was fortified with vast outworks of defence in the savage forests, marshes, and mountains that encompassed her, where the thoroughfares were streams choked with fallen trees and obstructed by cataracts. Never was the problem of moving troops encumbered

by artillery and baggage a more difficult one. The question was less how to fight an enemy than how to get at him.

It was just this problem which Amherst's industry and perseverance had power to solve. We read of his launching forth on to Lake George with a flotilla of eight hundred boats and an army of eleven thousand men, and all sounds simple and straightforward enough. Yet these boats, setting aside the original task of building and collecting them, had to make several journeys to carry the necessary stores and provisions from Albany to the head of the lake, while every one of them, together with its load, required to be hauled overland from three to six miles through forest and swamp from the carrying-place on the Mohawk to Wood Creek. The same provision against the same difficulties were necessary on a smaller scale for Prideaux's attack on Niagara, and, under conditions of special embarrassment, for Stanwix's advance to the Ohio; while over and above this, there was marine transport and all necessaries for the expedition to Quebec to be provided, so as to enable Wolfe to proceed on his mission fully equipped and without delay. Add to this burden of work endless correspondence with the various provinces, as well as constant friction, obstruction, and general dilatoriness, and it becomes apparent that for all his slowness Amherst accomplished no small feat when he achieved the conquest of Canada in two campaigns.

The whole problem was in truth one of organisation, and Amherst was the man to solve it, for he was a great military administrator. Cautious undoubtedly he was in the field, but it would be absurd to contend that a man who took ten thousand men down the rapids of the St. Lawrence, with the dry comment that the said rapids were "more frightful than dangerous,"[2] was wanting in enterprise or audacity. His career as a general in the field was short, and his crowning campaign, having achieved its end without a general action, has little fame.

Such is the penalty of bloodless operations, though they be the masterpiece of a mighty genius. Austerlitz is a name familiar to thousands who know nothing of the capitulation of Ulm. So Amherst to the majority of Englishmen is but a name: as though it were a small thing for a colonel taken straight from the classic fields of Flanders to cross the Atlantic to a savage wilderness, assume command of disheartened troops and the direction of discordant colonists, and quietly and deliberately to organise victory. He was the greatest military ad-

2. Amherst to Pitt, 8th Sept. 1760.

ministrator produced by England since the death of Marlborough, and remained the greatest until the rise of Wellington.

CHAPTER 21

The Battle of Bushy Run

An empire had been won: there remained the task of providing for its administration and for its defence. The gain in mere territory was in itself stupendous; and, though much of it might be but thinly populated, yet new territory necessarily implied new subjects. Apart from India, where, as shall be told in its place, the work of conquest had not been bounded by the expulsion of the French, the Spaniard required to be conciliated anew in Minorca; while in the West Indies, and still more in Canada and Florida, there were not only French and Spanish Colonists that must be absorbed, but large tribes of Indians, formerly dependent upon them, who must be summoned suddenly to cancel ancient treaties and friendships, and, though themselves un-conquered, to transfer their amity to the nation that had vanquished their former allies.

Nor was this all. In the West Indies and North America alike the newly acquired possessions lay alongside of clusters of British com-munities, which, though in the Caribbean Sea divided by but a few leagues of salt water and on the continent actually contiguous with each other, were riven asunder by passionate local and commercial jealousy. There was not one of these communities, not even the tiniest of the Antilles, but possessed its little legislature on the English model, and consequently not one but enjoyed facilities for excessive indul-gence of local feeling, local faction, and local folly, to the obstruction of all broad measures of Imperial policy. Never yet had it been pos-sible to combine the whole of the American provinces for common defence, even when the enemy was assailing their frontiers; never yet had the Leeward Islands suffered from a foreign foe, but Barbados had rejoiced over the weakening of a commercial rival. Thus the unifica-tion of the Old Empire, at any rate for purposes of defence, called as urgently for accomplishment as the incorporation of the new.

Such unity as the Empire had hitherto enjoyed was due to three principal causes: common attachment to the Crown as representing the mother country, common recourse to the mother country for protection, and common submission, which was rather nominal than real, to a commercial code imposed by the mother country. Thus there was one tie of sentiment, a second of interest, and a third which was entirely artificial and which might prove, if highly tested, to be opposed alike to interest and sentiment.

As to the first of these ties it is difficult, from the nature of the case, to speak with any precision; but there can be no doubt that there was in the Colonies at large a strong traditional attachment to the Crown, and, at the close of the Seven Years' War, a genuine pride in the prowess of the British arms and in the extension of the British dominions. Had King George the Second lived for another ten years, it is likely that the loyal affection of the British beyond sea would have centred itself about his person. As matters stood, it fastened itself with unerring instinct upon the great though now discarded minister, William Pitt; that is to say, upon the head of a party and not upon the head of the State. But it must never be forgotten that the large measure of self-government vouchsafed to one and all of the Colonies from their foundation could not but foster continually a spirit of independence; and this spirit had displayed itself at critical times in the most unexpected quarters.

The early assumption of independent sovereignty by the New England provinces, and in particular by Massachusetts is generally known; but it is less generally known that at the Revolution of 1688 such tiny communities as the Island of Nevis and the Bermudas had also attempted to put on the airs and graces of independent republics.[1] It must also be borne in mind that the chief delight of every Colonial Assembly lay in thwarting, in season or out of season, the representative of the Crown in the person of the governor.

In truth, the sentiment that is strongest in the colonist of Anglo-Saxon race is that of attachment to the land wherein he has made his home. This may still be found flourishing exuberantly in such unpromising soil as the tropical islet, where the white man's offspring is pale, sickly, and listless, and the black man's progeny alone can thrive and increase; much more must it abound in vast continents or great

---

1. *Cal. S. P. Col.*, 1689-1692, Governor Codrington's letters, and the Bermuda papers.

islands, where the white man can see his children and his children's children growing up in health and vigour, spreading further and further over forest and plain, past mountain and river, insatiable till they reach the Briton's true boundary, the sea.

As a rule very little romance is to be found in the settler of a new country, and such as there is reaches not to the little group of islands, called the British, in Western Europe, not to the noble minsters which recall the birth of their civilisation, nor to the ancient cities which were the cradles of their freedom. The heart of the colonist goes out to the natural grandeur of his own possessions, to the great forests which would hide whole English counties, to the huge trees which dwarf the British oak to insignificance, to the broad rivers which humble historic Thames to a rivulet, to the snow-capped mountains which bring low such paltry heights as Snowdon. To the European romance is of the past; to the colonist it is of the present and future. The citizen of the old world looks down on the pioneer of the new as provincial; and the officers of Braddock and Amherst in America had carried this spirit of condescension to a height which provoked just and natural resentment. But be the mother country never so perfectly maternal, loyal sentiment is and must be powerless against local attachment in a colony.

Strengthening the doubtful bond of sentiment there was the tie of interest. In the days of the Protectorate and of the Protestant Revolution even the West Indies had been able to furnish levies of white men not only for their own protection, but also for attack upon the French and Spanish Islands; but this old order had speedily passed away, and there had not yet arisen the new system of forming permanent regiments of negroes. So for two full generations the brunt of the fighting ashore in the Caribbean Archipelago had fallen upon British troops, while the dominant factor had been, as it still is, the British Fleet. In North America, New England had long striven to dispense with British protection, and, as has been told, had early taken the offensive unaided against the French in Canada; but she had been obliged to invoke the help of the mother country; and the final expulsion of the French had been achieved only by uniting to the colonial forces the full strength, both in Europe and America, of the British Army and the British Fleet.

For the aid thus granted and for the success thus gained, Massachusetts, the chief of the New England States, had thanked the king in effusive terms, adding, doubtless with sincerity at the moment, that the people would show their gratitude by every possible testimony of loyalty and of duty. But gratitude is one thing and interest is another. Moreover, the Americans had taken a full share in the peril of the fighting and in the glory of the conquest—a fact which was full of significance, for young communities, like young hounds, must be blooded before they can take their place in the pack of nations. The deliverance of the American provinces from their dangerous neighbour in Canada—a neighbour whose presence had haunted New England night and day for a century—freed them, as they supposed, from all internal peril. For deliverance from external foes they relied on the British Fleet; and, since the French had now no naval station on the North American coast, it was evident that any hostile operations of France against the continent must be beset by almost insuperable difficulties.

Quebec, the most inviting point for a French attack, was held by a British garrison; and at New York also there was a small body of regular troops, paid by Great Britain, as a nucleus for defence. Spain, it is true, held New Orleans and Havana, but no Anglo-Saxon treated Spain seriously as a naval power; and, with the whole breadth of the Atlantic Ocean between them and any probable enemy, the Americans were not far wrong in considering themselves invulnerable. Thus the tie of interest, though as strong as ever in the West Indies, was seriously weakened in North America.

Finally, there was the artificial tie of commercial legislation. By the Acts of Trade and Navigation the trade of the British Empire was restricted to vessels built in British dominions and manned, in very large proportion, by British subjects, which was fair enough; but, besides this, certain enumerated articles of commerce were forbidden to pass between foreign countries and British Colonies except by way of England, while rigorous legislation prohibited all manufactures in the Colonies which could possibly compete with those of England. On the other hand, Englishmen were equally interdicted from the purchase of any tobacco except that grown in British Colonies; while bounties on certain colonial products and the favouring of others to the prejudice of foreign powers, went very far towards balancing the scale of advantage and disadvantage between Mother Country and Colonies.

Such regulations, selfish though they might be, were the rule in those days, and must not be too hardly judged; but it is to be noted that they were purely commercial, and contained no suggestion whatever of a fund for Imperial defence. [2]

It need hardly be said that these restrictions on trade were absolutely impossible of enforcement. Many of them were winked at with the connivance of the authorities, and the whole of them were from the first evaded by a gigantic and scarcely concealed system of smuggling. In Great Britain the chief duty of troops in time of peace was the protection of revenue officers and reinforcement of the preventive service; and a sufficiently dangerous duty it frequently proved to be. The Isle of Man was described by Burke as a citadel of smuggling, and, when it was annexed to the Crown in 1762, it was found necessary to overawe it immediately by a squadron of light dragoons. On the immense Atlantic coast-line of America and in the West Indian Islands, where there was practically no preventive service, smuggling had flourished virtually unchecked for more than a century; and probably it was as well that this should have been so, for the Colonies would otherwise have been in a state of chronic rebellion.

In many of the provinces and islands there was hardly a man, from the governor downwards, who was not more or less interested in this illicit traffic; for it is the supreme danger of smuggling on a large scale that it involves the whole population, consciously or unconsciously, in violation of the law. [3] It may justly be pleaded that laws to impose artificial restraints on trade are an evil; but from violation of a bad law to general contempt of all law is but a very short step, especially where, as was the case in the Colonies, the executive is dangerously weak.

Thus, then, stood the relations between the mother country and the American Colonies at the close of the Seven Years' War. The tie of sentiment was strengthened for the moment by gratitude and pride, but the tie of interest was weakened by the expulsion of the French from Canada and by the oversetting of what was called the balance of power in America. There remained the tie of commercial legislation; and it is significant that as early as in 1761, after the fall of Montreal but before the conclusion of peace, James Otis, a lawyer of Boston, had lifted himself into prominence by a violent attack upon the entire commercial code. Herein it is true that he was guided at first by pri-

---

2. In Barbados and the Leeward Islands, the local Assemblies had indeed granted a duty on exports in perpetuity so far back as in the reign of Charles the Second, on condition that the proceeds should be devoted to local defence; but this formed no part of the commercial code.

3. Thus Governor Nicholson of Maryland, in 1695, described some of the leading inhabitants as "honest men, except in the matter of illegal trade."

vate animosity alone, but the proceeding was ominous; for the close of a great war, as the Peace of Ryswick had shown, is always a dangerous period, when politicians and agitators, who have been long thrust to the wall by generals and admirals, return again to their places with louder voices and enhanced importance.

For Britain itself, of course, the same critical moment had come. At a time when the high problem of Imperial defence seemed likely to prove insoluble, except as part of the still higher problem of Imperial union, the country was torn by factions innumerable. Bute, albeit the most unpopular man in England, remained in office until April 1763; but though there was enough against him as an individual, the bitterest reproach levelled at him was that he was a Scotsman; and hence there arose a rage against the sister kingdom which was as mischievous as it was unworthy.

On the other side, the once powerful Whig party was split up into four or more sections, owing to the petty jealousies of the leading Whig families; while Pitt, the only commanding figure among a host of pygmies, stood moody and implacable aloof. At a time when all public men should have been working together to secure the vast possessions acquired during the war, and to lighten the burden of debt which was one of its inevitable bequests, they were squabbling, intriguing, and caballing for their own supposed interests, forgetful of their country and of the Empire which was committed to their care. Abroad, England had not a friend in Europe. France and Spain, humiliated by defeat and loss of territory, awaited only the moment for taking their revenge. Frederick the Great, unmindful of the help that he had received, and remembering only that of which he had been disappointed, lay like some surly old dog, licking his wounds and growling as he thought how he had received them. No more unpromising time could have been conceived for the inception of a task that demanded the highest constructive statesmanship.

As must needs be at the close of every war, Bute's first duty was the reduction of the army to peace-establishment, which was effected by disbanding or dooming to disbandment all Infantry of the Line junior to the Seventieth Foot, and all Cavalry junior to the Eighteenth Light Dragoons. [4] The establishment for Great Britain was fixed at seventeen thousand five hundred men, including nearly three thousand Invalids; that for the Colonies at ten thousand men; and that for Minorca and

---

4. This regiment was disbanded in 1821, but its honours have been transferred to the present Eighteenth Hussars, which was raised in 1858.

Gibraltar at rather more than four thousand men; which, with eighteen hundred artillery, and the invariable twelve thousand men on the Irish establishment, made up a total of rather more than forty-five thousand men in all. It was a paltry handful of troops to guard so vast an Empire, with its many important naval stations; and the king's speech explained that the reorganised militia was counted upon to secure the safety of Great Britain. [5]

Yet it was less the weakness than the undue strength of the Army which met with reprobation from men of repute for wisdom. Edmund Burke wrote in 1774 of the "huge increase of the military establishment" at the peace, and regarded twenty new regiments only as twenty fresh colonels capable of holding seats in the House of Commons. The comment is typical of the spirit in which the question of defence was approached. It is an undoubted and lamentable fact that colonelcies of regiments were freely given as rewards for political service; but it is not difficult to show that Burke's contention was on the face of it childish. The foreign garrisons included Minorca, Gibraltar, Bermuda, the Bahamas, St. Vincent, Dominica, Tobago, Grenada and the Grenadines, Jamaica, New York, Halifax, Quebec, Mobile and Pensacola, besides a chain of posts extending for some three thousand miles from the St. Lawrence in the north to the lower Mississippi in the south of America. The whole of the West Indies were subject always to the danger of an insurrection either of negro slaves or of savage natives; while the entire western frontier of North America lay exposed to attack by Indians. Yet the huge force allotted for the protection of these possessions did not exceed fifteen thousand men.

Within a month of the voting of the new establishment, a sudden movement in America threw startling light on the vexed question of Colonial defence. It will be remembered that after the fall of Montreal in 1760, Major Rogers, the famous ranger, had been sent with a few troops to enforce the capitulation of the French posts on the great lakes and at the back of Canada. During his progress he was met by an Ottawa chief named Pontiac, who asked him what he did there, but, being answered that the French had surrendered the entire country to the English, seemed to acquiesce in the new state of affairs. None the less the whole of the Indian tribes were galled to the quick by the thought that the territory, which they claimed as their own, should have been transferred by one white nation to another, without a word

---

5. *C.J.* 19th April 1763.

of consultation with them.

French traders and French adventurers who had penetrated into these remote regions, where they lived a half-savage life among the native tribes, lost no opportunity of inflaming the resentment of the Indians against the British; while the British on their side took small pains to conciliate their new subjects. Finally Pontiac, who went near to be a man of genius, planned a great confederation of all the Indian tribes, to attack the whole of the British posts simultaneously and to drive the hated intruders, as his ignorant followers hoped, into the sea. His emissaries flew far and wide to the various chiefs, northward to the head of Lakes Michigan and Huron, southward to the very mouth of the Mississippi; and by the spring of 1763 the weapon of offence was forged and Pontiac ready to strike.

On the British side the chances of parrying such a blow were slender indeed. Amherst's force had been reduced to a mere skeleton by the costly expeditions to Martinique and to Havana; thousands of men had died, and as many thousands had been rendered unserviceable by sickness. The consequence was that the posts for securing the Indian territory were held with ridiculous weakness, though there was hardly one of them within distance to support another. Beginning at Niagara and following the southern shore of Lake Erie, there came in succession Forts Presquile, Le Boeuf, and Sandusky; while Fort Detroit guarded the passage to Lake Huron, and Michillimackinac, now called by the shorter name of Mackinaw, the strait between Huron and Michigan, with a small outpost, Sault St. Marie, on the straits between Lakes Huron and Superior a few miles to northward. In the southeast corner of Lake Michigan stood Fort St. Joseph, a connecting link with Ouatanon on the Wabash, while Fort Miamis on the Maumee preserved communication between Ouatanon and Lake Erie. Finally, there was the chain of posts on the line from Pennsylvania to the Ohio, Forts Cumberland, Bedford, Ligonier, and Pitt, all of them familiar to us since the days of Braddock, with Fort Venango northward of Fort Pitt, to secure the passage to Presquile and Niagara.

The garrisons of these stations were formed almost entirely by the Sixtieth or Royal American Regiment, a corps which was still composed in great measure of foreigners, both officers and men. A dreary life these detachments led in the wilderness, hundreds of miles from any civilised settlement, ill-fed, ill-provided, ill-cared-for—in a word, forgotten. One poor German from Presquile, in quaint misspelled English wrote:

We have no kint of flesh nor vension nor fish, and that we could suffer with patience; but the porck is so bad that neither officers nor men can eat it . . . and self lief (I myself have lived) more than seventeen weeks upon flour and peace-soup, and have eat no kint of meat but a little bear at Christmas.

An English officer from Ligonier wrote:

My garrison consists of Rodgers, unfit for any kind of fatigue, Davis, improper to be entrusted on any duty, Shillem, quite a little boy, my servant, an inactive simple creature . . . and one more. Two stout fellows would beat the whole five of them. [6]

Lonely and friendless, the officers took to themselves Indian girls for companions, a practice which, whatever judgment be passed on it, was destined to prove the salvation of the British.

On the 7th of May 1763, Pontiac and sixty other chiefs entered Fort Detroit, the strongest of all the posts, ostensibly for friendly conference with the *commandant*, Captain Gladwyn, but every man with a weapon under his blanket ready for a treacherous attack. Gladwyn, warned by his Indian girl, was on his guard and able to frustrate the whole plot, but foolishly let the chiefs go instead of keeping them as hostages; and three days later the fort was beset on every side by some six hundred Indians. Gladwyn, though he had provisions for but three weeks, held out stoutly, and by the help of a friendly French settler contrived to replenish his stores. He had but six score of regular soldiers, besides some forty traders and half-breeds, who were by no means implicitly to be trusted; but he thrust arms into the hands of all, and stood vigorously at bay. Meanwhile, from all quarters came tidings of disaster.

On the 16th of May Sandusky fell, and the entire garrison was killed or taken; on the 25th the like fate befell Fort St. Joseph; and on the 28th a relieving force of one hundred men, with stores and ammunition from Niagara, was cut to pieces within a day's march of Detroit. The fall of Fort Miamis, of Presquile, Le Boeuf, Venango, Ouatanon, and Mackinaw, followed hard upon these in the last days of May and the first days of June, some few, but very few, of the men escaping. Sault St. Marie and another outlying post were evacuated; and by the middle of June there was not a British soldier in the region

6. Ensign Schlösser to Bouquet, 24th January 1762; Blane to Bouquet, 5th May 1762. *Add. MS.*, 21648.

of the Lakes except at Detroit. Hideous though were the scenes of massacre and torture, it is impossible not to admire, from a military standpoint, the masterly swiftness and precision of Pontiac's stroke.

On the route from Pennsylvania to the Ohio, however, Forts Pitt, Ligonier, and Bedford repelled the Indian attacks; while Gladwyn, though the number of his besiegers had been augmented fivefold by the fall of the neighbouring posts, had received a reinforcement of some sixty men, with stores and ammunition, and more than held his own. A second reinforcement of some men of the Fifty-Fifth and of Gorham's Rangers, under Major Rogers, also found its way to him at the end of July; and, though he narrowly escaped disaster by attempting a sortie, he had, with a force of three hundred men, little to fear.

The first violence of the storm had spent itself, and the British had gained a little breathing-time. Amherst, at first incredulous of the extent of the mischief, and unduly contemptuous of his enemy, had already set himself to arrange for the despatch of a relieving force; but despite the urgency of the danger, he was cruelly hampered by want of men. Though the posts between Pennsylvania and the Ohio still held out, the whole of the country between them was laid waste; while the forts themselves were crowded with refugees, who waited only for rumour to revive fresh panic in them before they fled away in wild terror to eastward.

Fort Ligonier was held by but twelve soldiers, yet not one of the flying settlers would remain to stand by them. Amherst early decided that his relieving column must move along the line of these forts, and with excellent judgment decided to place Colonel Bouquet in command; but in the dearth of regular troops he was fain to apply to Pennsylvania for local levies. It is hardly credible, but it is a fact, that even in the face of the deadly peril upon its borders the province refused to provide a man.

None the less, by the end of June Bouquet had with great difficulty assembled five hundred regular troops at Carlisle, designing to move from thence, by Forbes's route of 1758, upon Fort Pitt. His force consisted mainly of detachments of the Forty-second, Sixtieth, and Montgomery's Highlanders, strengthened by drafts from other corps; but, even so, many of Montgomery's were so much enfeebled by the West Indian campaign as to be quite unfit for duty, and no fewer than sixty, being unable to march, were carried in waggons to reinforce the posts on the way. Early orders had been given for the preparation of a convoy of provisions at Carlisle, but such was the terror inspired by

COLONEL BOUQUET AT A COUNCIL FIRE IN 1764

the Indian invasion that nothing had been done.

Eighteen days therefore were lost before Bouquet, having with much difficulty collected transport and supplies, began his march south-westward by Shippensburg upon Fort Bedford. Arrived there, he halted for three days, and had the good fortune during his stay to engage thirty backwoodsmen to accompany him; for though, ever since his coming to Carlisle, he had been besieged by refugees with terrible stories of massacre and destruction, not a man of them could be persuaded to join him. Thence pursuing his way by the rough track hewn by Forbes through the forest, he on the 2nd of August reached Fort Ligonier, fifty leagues from his starting-point; and leaving there his oxen and waggons, continued his march on the 4th with three hundred and fifty packhorses and a few driven cattle only. On that night he encamped but a few miles from Fort Ligonier, intending to start early next morning, push on as far as a stream called Bushy Run, rest there till night, and pass through the dangerous defile of Turtle Creek, which lay a short distance beyond it, under cover of darkness.

Early on the morning of the 5th, the troops moved off accordingly, over steep and broken ground shrouded everywhere by dense forest, and at one o'clock, after a tramp of seventeen miles, were approaching the appointed halting-place, when a sharp fire in the van told that the advanced guard was engaged. Two companies were at once sent forward, which, charging through the forest, speedily cleared the ground with the bayonet; but this was hardly accomplished before renewed firing showed that the Indians, true to their usual tactics, had developed a simultaneous attack on both flanks and in rear.

Bouquet thereupon recalled his men to protect his pack-horses, and formed the whole of his troops in a ring around them. The Indians attacked with great gallantry, charging again and again with wild yells up to the line, only to be driven back by steady and telling volleys. But the counter-attack of the bayonet was of little avail against so active an enemy in the forest; and the savages, skipping nimbly from tree to tree, kept themselves under cover, constantly changing the point of assault and pouring in always a destructive fire. For seven long hours the fight raged fiercely, until at nightfall the Indian fire at last slackened, and the weary soldiers enjoyed a little respite from the eternal rain of bullets. It was but a respite, for there was little rest for them that night. To move in the presence of such an enemy was impossible, so, though not a drop of water was within reach, the troops bivouacked where they stood, lying down in order of battle.

PLAN of the BATTLE near BUSHY-RUN,

Gained by Colonel Bouquet, over the
Delawares, Shawanese, Mingoes, Wyandots, Mohikons, Miamies, & Ottawas;
on the 5.th and 6.th of August 1763.
Survey'd by Thos. Hutchins, Assistant Engineer.

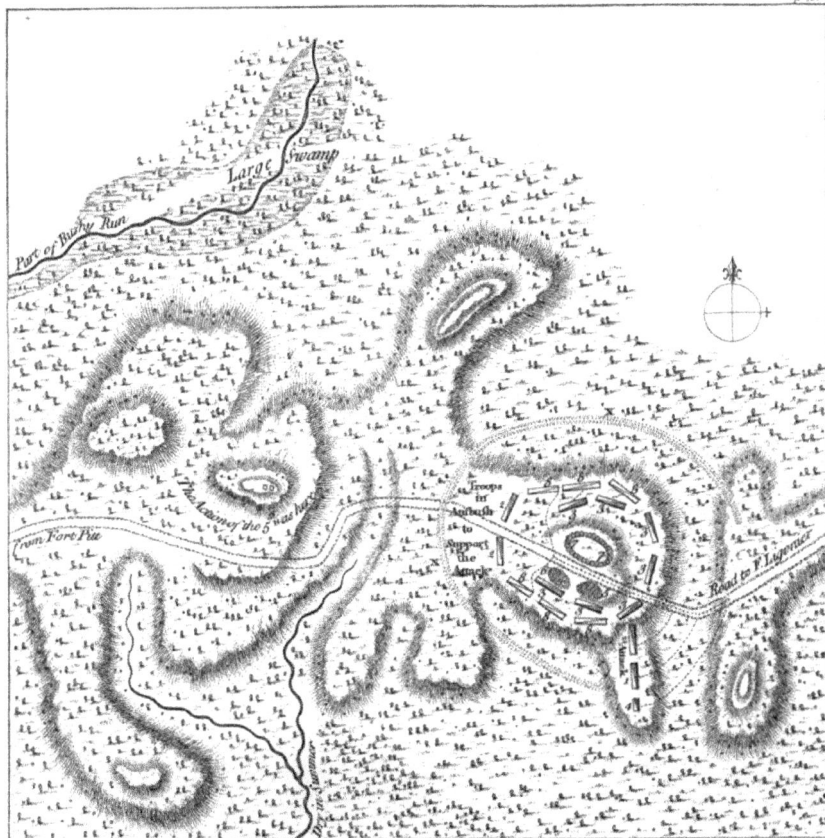

REFERENCES.

1. Grenadiers
2. Light Infantry
3. Battalion Men
4. Rangers
5. Cattle
6. Horses
7. Entrenchment of Bags for the Wounded
x. The Enemy
8. First Position of the Troops
o o Graves

Numerous outposts were pushed into the forest to guard against a night-attack; and in the centre of the bivouac a wall of flour-bags was thrown up as shelter for the wounded. In truth Bouquet's heart misgave him lest his force should share the fate of Braddock's. His losses had been severe, several officers and some sixty men having fallen killed or wounded; and he could feel no confidence in the issue of a combat on the morrow with his men worn out by fatigue, fighting, and thirst.

Throughout the night occasional whoops told of the presence of the enemy, and at the first glimmer of dawn the Indian attack was renewed, with the same deadly fire from unseen marksmen and the same furious rushes at point after point. The British still fought on bravely; but with renewed exertion and the increasing heat of the sun their thirst became intolerable. From time to time a mob of pack-horses, maddened by wounds, would break away from their place by the wall of flour-bags, crash through the fighting line, and scour away into the forest, while their drivers hid themselves in abject terror without an effort to control them. At ten o'clock the British, though thinned by heavy losses, still kept the ring unbroken, but began to waver from sheer exhaustion. Encouraged by these signs of weakness, the Indians attacked with fresh confidence; and as a last desperate resource Bouquet withdrew two companies into the interior of the bivouac, extending the files of the troops on each flank across the gap, as though to cover the retreat.

The Indians, now assured of victory, pressed furiously into the space thus weakened, and seemed to be on the point of carrying all before them, when they were staggered by a destructive volley full upon their flank. Bouquet, taking advantage of a fold in the ground, had sent the two withdrawn companies to fetch a compass through the forest; and these now opened their counter-attack. The Indians, though heavily punished, with great bravery wheeled to return the fire, but would not stand to await the bayonets that came charging upon them through the trees. They turned and fled in wild confusion; but Bouquet had not done with them yet. Two more companies had advanced by his order before the ring, and now lay in ambush ready for the fugitives. As the Indians passed them, these poured in a volley as destructive as that of their comrades, and the four companies uniting drove the savages through the forest without rest or respite, killing several and dispersing the rest. The Indians on the other side of the ring, seeing the rout of their fellows, did not await attack, but fled likewise; and in a short time the British stood alone upon the ground, every sign of a living Indian having vanished.

Around the ring lay the corpses of some sixty dead warriors, but Bouquet's loss was little less severe, amounting to eight officers and ninety-six men, or fully a fourth of his force, killed and wounded in the two days' fighting. The action was one of the fiercest ever fought with Indians; and had any man of less experience in such warfare than Bouquet been in command, its issue might well have been disastrous. Nothing but entire confidence in him, added to the dread of being roasted alive, could have kept the exhausted troops to their work; while the final stratagem whereby success was won reflects equal credit on the resource of the commander and the perfect steadiness of the men. Long though the combat has been forgotten in England, the history of the army can show few finer performances on its own scale than this victory of a handful of English, Highlanders, and Germans under the leadership of a Swiss colonel.

The result of the action was immediate, for the column reached Fort Pitt with little further opposition or loss on the 10th. There Bouquet left another officer in command and returned eastward for the further work that lay before him. A reinforcement of three hundred provincial rangers would have enabled him to finish the campaign there and then; but the Americans, who had not been ashamed to save themselves while British soldiers, too weak to stand on their legs, encountered their enemies, very consistently declined to furnish a man.

So far the depredations of the Indians had been confined to the remoter British posts and to the western borders of Virginia, Maryland, and Pennsylvania. The Iroquois, or Six Nations, who lay between Lake Ontario and New York, had for the most part been kept firm to the British alliance by the influence of Sir William Johnson, and only a single tribe, the Senecas, had thrown in their lot with Pontiac. These Senecas, however, with other insurgent tribes, wrought no little havoc on the western border of New York, and actually succeeded in surprising a convoy near Fort Niagara, and in destroying seventy out of eighty men of the escort. This in the existing scarcity of troops was a serious matter.

Detroit was still blockaded; and affairs were not improved when a force of six hundred regular soldiers, assembled with infinite difficulty at Niagara for its relief, was caught by a storm on Lake Erie and compelled to return with the loss of all stores and ammunition and of seventy men drowned. It was not until the end of October that

The Indians lay siege to Fort Detroit

Pontiac and his warriors broke up from before Detroit, and then not for military reasons, but in ostensible deference to orders from the French. The chief, however, withdrew only with full though secret intention to return.

Meanwhile Amherst, having again appealed to the provinces to call up levies for their defence, resigned his command and embarked for England, leaving the final suppression of the rising to his successor, General Gage. The Colonies returned no very willing response to his summons. Massachusetts and Connecticut; made their assistance conditional on a renewal of the war with the Western Indians; Rhode Island, always churlish, sent no answer whatever; New Hampshire was profuse in excuses; and only New York and New Jersey promised to furnish one thousand men between them, stipulating, however, that two-thirds of them should remain on their own frontiers. [7] Virginia had already sent a force to protect her outlying settlements; but Pennsylvania refused to vote her contingent of one thousand men, and even denounced an expedition, conducted voluntarily by some of her citizens against the Indians, as seditious and murderous. Nothing less than the march of a body of Pennsylvanian border-men, fully armed and equipped, upon Philadelphia, was necessary to awe the Quaker Assembly [8] into taking care for the defence of its own people. But by that time the season was too far spent for further operations, and it was plain that the complete subjugation of the Indians would require another campaign.

It was accordingly decided that, as soon as the spring of 1764 should permit, two separate columns should march, one under Bouquet from Fort Pitt into the settlements of the Delawares and Shawanoes, who were the soul of the insurrection, in the valley of the Ohio, and the other under Colonel Bradstreet from Albany, to quell the tribes about Detroit. Bradstreet, the hero of Fort Frontenac in 1758, was the first to move, with a force made up partly of regulars and partly of provincial levies; [9] but in spite of the fair promises of the previous year the entire provincial contingent did not exceed one thousand men, and those of very poor quality. The service, promising little honour or advantage, was naturally unpopular; and notwithstanding professions of zeal to

---

7. Gage to Halifax, 10th March, 12th May 1764.

8. The study of our early colonial history is a severe trial to any man who desires to hold the sect of Quakers in respect.

9. New York troops, 500; New Jersey and Connecticut, 500; H.M. 17th and Gage's Light Infantry, and Royal Artillery with ten guns. Gage to Halifax, 12th May 1764.

encounter internal enemies, the provinces took little pains to encourage men to enlist.

There is little worth narrating of the expedition itself, for Bradstreet, though he duly relieved Detroit and reoccupied Sandusky and Mackinaw, disobeyed his orders to punish the offending tribes, and contented himself with accepting vain promises and concluding fallacious treaties with his enemy. By November he had returned to Niagara, having accomplished nothing, but added rather to the difficulties of Bouquet's column.

Bouquet meanwhile had undergone the common fate of British commanders who relied on provincial levies. Virginia and Maryland flatly refused to send him a man; and a contingent of one thousand men, which had at last been wrung from Pennsylvania, was not ready to move until July, by which time the season for navigation of the Ohio was past. However, on the 5th of August he reached Carlisle with his provincials and a detachment of the Forty-Second and Sixtieth, for the most part veterans of Bushy Run.

Within five days two hundred of the Pennsylvanians had deserted, and Bouquet was obliged to beg for Virginians to fill their place; but none the less he continued his march, reaching Fort Pitt on the 17th of September with no further loss than that of another hundred Pennsylvanian deserters. Here he picked up a welcome reinforcement of Virginian backwoodsmen, and marching again at the beginning of October entered a wilderness never before trodden by an army. Advancing with every precaution, he made his way steadily southwestward for one hundred miles into the heart of the Delaware and Shawanoe settlements on the River Muskingum. The moral effect of his invasion and a little well-timed severity accomplished the object of the campaign without the firing of a shot, and Bouquet returned to Carlisle with a difficult task well done.

From that time, although there was still to be a little trouble before the posts on the Illinois could be occupied, the power of the Indian conspiracy was broken. have dwelt, it may seem, with undue fullness upon certain details of these campaigns, but not without a purpose. It is no more than the truth to say that the brunt of this most dangerous and trying warfare had fallen wholly upon the king's troops. It was they who held Detroit; it was on them, in their miserable ruined forts, that the refugees of Pennsylvania had rallied for a time; it was they who fought and won the action of Bushy Run, saving the province from horrors untold; it was they who formed the backbone of the force that marched to the Muskingum; finally, by a strange irony, it was they whom the panic-stricken burghers of Philadelphia had summoned (though they could not be spared) for defence against the righteous indignation of their own people. It might have been supposed that the harried provinces of Virginia and Maryland would have felt gratitude to Bouquet for their deliverance; but it was not so.

Virginia refused to pay the volunteers that had accompanied him to the Muskingum, and tried hard to fasten the cost upon the colonel himself. He was only relieved, after endless annoyance and vexation, by the Assembly of Pennsylvania, which made tardy amends for past shortcomings by undertaking to supply the necessary moneys. The gallant man did not long survive this last campaign, for within three years he died at Pensacola, having first received promotion to the rank of brigadier for his services; and it can only be said that the end of his career was not untimely. The only conclusion that could be drawn from the attitude of the Colonies towards him was that they would take no burden upon themselves which they could lay upon the British soldier that in fact they would even allow sick Highlanders to be dragged out of hospital to the front to defend able-bodied Americans. Such a spirit was not encouraging for a happy solution of the problem of Imperial defence.

LEONAUR

ALSO FROM LEONAUR
AVAILABLE IN SOFTCOVER OR HARDCOVER WITH DUST JACKET

IRON TIMES WITH THE GUARDS *by An O. E. (G. P. A. Fildes)*—The Experiences of an Officer of the Coldstream Guards on the Western Front During the First World War.

THE GREAT WAR IN THE MIDDLE EAST: 1 *by W. T. Massey*—The Desert Campaigns & How Jerusalem Was Won---two classic accounts in one volume.

THE GREAT WAR IN THE MIDDLE EAST: 2 *by W. T. Massey*—Allenby's Final Triumph.

SMITH-DORRIEN *by Horace Smith-Dorrien*—Isandlwhana to the Great War.

1914 *by Sir John French*—The Early Campaigns of the Great War by the British Commander.

GRENADIER *by E. R. M. Fryer*—The Recollections of an Officer of the Grenadier Guards throughout the Great War on the Western Front.

BATTLE, CAPTURE & ESCAPE *by George Pearson*—The Experiences of a Canadian Light Infantryman During the Great War.

DIGGERS AT WAR *by R. Hugh Knyvett & G. P. Cuttriss*—"Over There" With the Australians by R. Hugh Knyvett and Over the Top With the Third Australian Division by G. P. Cuttriss. Accounts of Australians During the Great War in the Middle East, at Gallipoli and on the Western Front.

HEAVY FIGHTING BEFORE US *by George Brenton Laurie*—The Letters of an Officer of the Royal Irish Rifles on the Western Front During the Great War.

THE CAMELIERS *by Oliver Hogue*—A Classic Account of the Australians of the Imperial Camel Corps During the First World War in the Middle East.

RED DUST *by Donald Black*—A Classic Account of Australian Light Horsemen in Palestine During the First World War.

THE LEAN, BROWN MEN *by Angus Buchanan*—Experiences in East Africa During the Great War with the 25th Royal Fusiliers—the Legion of Frontiersmen.

THE NIGERIAN REGIMENT IN EAST AFRICA *by W. D. Downes*—On Campaign During the Great War 1916-1918.

THE 'DIE-HARDS' IN SIBERIA *by John Ward*—With the Middlesex Regiment Against the Bolsheviks 1918-19.

LEONAUR

ALSO FROM LEONAUR
AVAILABLE IN SOFTCOVER OR HARDCOVER WITH DUST JACKET

FARAWAY CAMPAIGN *by F. James*—Experiences of an Indian Army Cavalry Officer in Persia & Russia During the Great War.

REVOLT IN THE DESERT *by T. E. Lawrence*—An account of the experiences of one remarkable British officer's war from his own perspective.

MACHINE-GUN SQUADRON *by A. M. G.*—The 20th Machine Gunners from British Yeomanry Regiments in the Middle East Campaign of the First World War.

A GUNNER'S CRUSADE *by Antony Bluett*—The Campaign in the Desert, Palestine & Syria as Experienced by the Honourable Artillery Company During the Great War .

DESPATCH RIDER *by W. H. L. Watson*—The Experiences of a British Army Motorcycle Despatch Rider During the Opening Battles of the Great War in Europe.

TIGERS ALONG THE TIGRIS *by E. J. Thompson*—The Leicestershire Regiment in Mesopotamia During the First World War.

HEARTS & DRAGONS *by Charles R. M. F. Crutwell*—The 4th Royal Berkshire Regiment in France and Italy During the Great War, 1914-1918.

INFANTRY BRIGADE: 1914 *by John Ward*—The Diary of a Commander of the 15th Infantry Brigade, 5th Division, British Army, During the Retreat from Mons.

DOING OUR 'BIT' *by Ian Hay*—Two Classic Accounts of the Men of Kitchener's 'New Army' During the Great War including *The First 100,000* & *All In It*.

AN EYE IN THE STORM *by Arthur Ruhl*—An American War Correspondent's Experiences of the First World War from the Western Front to Gallipoli-and Beyond.

STAND & FALL *by Joe Cassells*—With the Middlesex Regiment Against the Bolsheviks 1918-19.

RIFLEMAN MACGILL'S WAR *by Patrick MacGill*—A Soldier of the London Irish During the Great War in Europe including *The Amateur Army*, *The Red Horizon* & *The Great Push*.

WITH THE GUNS *by C. A. Rose & Hugh Dalton*—Two First Hand Accounts of British Gunners at War in Europe During World War 1- Three Years in France with the Guns and With the British Guns in Italy.

THE BUSH WAR DOCTOR *by Robert V. Dolbey*—The Experiences of a British Army Doctor During the East African Campaign of the First World War.